I'm Glad I'm a Mom

JILL SAVAGE
General Editor

HARVEST HOUSE PUBLISHERS

EUGENE, OREGON

Cover by Garborg Design Works, Savage, Minnesota

Cover photos © iStockphoto

Published in association with the literary agency of Alive Communications, Inc., 7680 Goddard Street, Ste #200, Colorado Springs, CO 80920, www.alivecommunications.com

I'M GLAD I'M A MOM
Copyright © 2008 by Hearts at Home®
Published by Harvest House Publishers
Eugene, Oregon 97402
www.harvesthousepublishers.com

Library of Congress Cataloging-in-Publication Data
I'm glad I'm a mom / Jill Savage, general editor.
   p. cm.
   ISBN-13: 978-0-7369-2381-1 (pbk.)
   ISBN-10: 0-7369-2381-0 (pbk.)
   1. Mothers—Religious life. 2. Mothers—Anecdotes. I. Savage, Jill, 1964-
BV4529.18.I4 2008
248.8'431—dc22
                                                                        2007041003

Printed in the United States of America

08 09 10 11 12 13 14 15 16 / VP-SK / 12 11 10 9 8 7 6 5 4 3 2 1

Special thanks to:

All the women who shared their stories and joined the mission of Hearts at Home by encouraging other moms!

The publications team of Hearts at Home, who lovingly quilted this book together. Especially Megan Kaeb, Mary Steinke, Terri Thede, Carmen Peterson, Mycah Amstutz, Julie Kaiser, and Kelly Hughes.

All of the Hearts at Home staff who have helped with this project in direct and indirect ways and who continue to work selflessly creating events and resources that encourage, educate, and equip moms.

Beth Jusino, our wise and supportive literary agent, who guided our processes and suggested this resource.

Our friends at Harvest House. It is truly a privilege to partner with you in this ministry.

And to moms everywhere. Your job is more important than you may ever know! May this book assure you that you are not alone and encourage you as you navigate the joys and challenges of motherhood!

Contents

Section Four: Decisions, Dilemmas, and Determination

Section Five: Faith of a Child

Section Six: Muddling Through Mistakes and Mishaps

Section Seven: God-Touches in the Trenches

Foreword

I live in Normal, Illinois. Yes, there really is such a place. And yes, we get all the jokes about being "normal" or "abnormal" in this place called Normal.

Yet even living in a place called Normal, there have been times when I've wondered if I am normal. Are my experiences normal? Are my children normal? Are the struggles I'm going through in my marriage normal? Are my emotions normal? What about this feeling of being overwhelmed...is that normal?

When I joined my first moms group, I experienced honest conversation about the realities of mothering, marriage, and homemaking. I found out that I wasn't as alone as I thought I was. And do you know what? I found out that I am normal! In that mothering community I found perspective, hope, and encouragement, as well as other women who understood what my life is like.

Years later my Mom2Mom group started Hearts at Home, an organization designed to encourage, educate, and equip women in the profession of mothering. Through books like this, our bi-monthly magazine, our website, and our conference events, we help "normalize" real-life experiences for moms. After 15 years of mothering conferences, not a year goes by without a mom communicating that she was crying within the first few minutes of a Hearts at Home conference. Most are caught off guard by this unexpected emotion, but later realize it's the result of understanding they are normal. What a mix of gratitude, relief, and encouragement that provides!

This book is designed to help you know that you are normal. These are stories written by real moms who are in the trenches of everyday life just like you: diapers, dishes, preschool, carpools, and even cheering from the bleachers. No matter what season of motherhood you are in, you'll find experiences similar to your own and personal insights that will warm your heart. These slice-of-life true stories are honest, heartfelt, and often humorous. By illuminating the dark places in our life where we are absolutely sure "no one has ever felt this way before," these stories move you and me from isolation to community.

I believe this book will affirm you. It will give you hope. It will lend you perspective. It will even help you know you're not crazy. More than anything, it will allow you to spend time with other women who understand what your life is like.

Welcome to normal! I think it's a great place to live!

Jill Savage
Mother of Five
Founder and Executive Director, Hearts at Home

Expect the Unexpected

1

Lost in Translation

by Liz Curtis Higgs

My teenage daughter loves the Far East—the clothes, the artwork, the culture, the music, the anime, the manga, the whole bit. Anything marked "Made in Japan" makes her heart sing.

When it came time to shop for her school's Winter Ball—a formal affair, one notch down from a prom—she found the Oriental dress of her dreams online. Not your typical brightly hued gown made of slinky material with lots of straps and slits, but a genuine cheongsam. You've seen them: long, straight silk brocade dresses with short capped sleeves and frog closures.

Who was I to argue with so classic—and modest—a design?

My daughter's favorite cheongsam was pale lavender—the perfect color for her, and at a price almost too good to be true. A few days before Christmas I ordered the dress in her size, certain we'd receive it in time for her January dance. Though imported from China, the item was definitely in stock and already in the States.

My daughter was thrilled. The perfect dress!

Mom was even more elated. No trip to the mall!

One full week went by. Not long for mail order, but too long for my daughter.

"Please e-mail the company!" she begged, which I dutifully did in

13

apologetic tones. "I know it's been only seven days, but I thought I'd see how things were looking…"

Things were looking good. Mere hours later, we heard back from them: "Gown on way. You receive soon." Not the detailed delivery information I'd hoped for, but still encouraging.

Another anxious week of awaiting a delivery truck, and still no big brown box.

My daughter was not the only one getting desperate. I dreaded the thought of a last-minute shopping debacle, filled with high expectations and zero success. We had *so* been there in seasons past. And my husband, Bill—forced to endure all this female angst—was losing patience fast.

I e-mailed the company again, wording my request more tersely this time: (1) How was it shipped? (2) Do you have a tracking number? (3) When can we expect delivery?

Once again, a speedy reply came via e-mail. "Already sent. Please wait few more days."

Alas, we didn't *have* a few more days.

This was Thursday. The Winter Ball was Friday. My daughter and I (please help us, Lord) were bound for the mall.

We dragged ourselves out the door, both miserable. She had her heart set on *that* gown. I just wanted *a* gown without all the department store drama.

Could we keep from losing patience with each other *and* find a dress? I prayed for a minor miracle as we climbed into our seldom-used second car.

A pile of mail rested on the passenger side. "Good grief," I muttered, noticing the late-December postmarks. "Your father must have pulled this stuff out of our mailbox ten days ago!" I collected the letters and catalogs, intending to throw them in the backseat, when a manila envelope caught my eye.

It couldn't be. But it was.

Out of a plain, flat, hand-addressed 9 x 12 envelope—no padding, no wrapping—fell my daughter's silk dress.

"Wheee!" she shrieked, dashing in the house to try it on, her stunned mother trailing after her.

Ten days of worrying. Ten days of whining. Ten days of a slender package quietly waiting in our driveway because *Bill forgot to bring in the mail!*

I didn't know whether to laugh, cry, or wring my dear husband's neck.

Our daughter, meanwhile, was doing pirouettes around the house in her new dress. "This was *supposed* to happen, Mom. I need to learn not to care so much about material stuff."

Did my daughter actually say that? She did. Life lessons come in the strangest packages—and land in the oddest places.

Did I strangle my husband when he got home? I did not. In our 20 years of marriage I, too, have forgotten things. Misplaced things. Just plain *lost* things.

Only one challenge remained (other than choosing the right shoes). What was I going to say to those kind people at the Chinese import company?

Dear Sirs:
So very sorry to have troubled you!
The dress got lost in the mail…

*L*iz Curtis Higgs is the bestselling author of *Bad Girls of the Bible, The Pumpkin Patch Parable, Thorn in My Heart,* and two dozen other books, and she has presented 1500 inspirational programs for audiences worldwide. She lives with her husband and two grown children in Kentucky. Visit her website: www.LizCurtisHiggs.com.

2

Chow Down

by Leslie Wilson

People are supposed to eat people food, right?

Not always, according to what I've witnessed.

A few weeks ago, my daughter Molly had two friends over to spend the night. The girls watched movies, played Twister, and giggled in my daughter's room all evening. They emerged only for food and drink—and candy. An unexplained prodding prompted me to check on them while they snacked in our kitchen.

As I entered, three dark blond heads jerked toward me, visibly startled. Molly flashed me a plastic smile. "We're just having a little snack."

Each girl had a single-serving cup of applesauce—with something mixed in.

"What are those lumps in the applesauce?"

"Uh…" Molly hesitated, glancing at her friends for moral support. They stared back blankly, as if to say, "Hey, she's *your* mom."

I repeated the question, stepping closer to the chopping block, surrounded on three sides by budding chef-scientists.

"We mixed cat food in the applesauce," Molly admitted, obviously holding her breath to read my reaction.

"What?" I squeaked, my voice like a boy in the throes of puberty. "You're eating cat food?"

"Morgan's parents let her," Molly patiently explained.

"So?" I shrilled, shaking my head back and forth in disbelief and disgust.

"Well, I didn't think you'd mind..." Molly's voice trailed off, as it dawned on her that, in fact, I *did* mind. "Do you not want us to eat this?"

Okay, good. She was finally getting it.

"No, it's gross!" Sensing I needed to soften my tone, I tried again. "Look, I don't have to worry about Morgan's parents, but I don't want to be known as the mom who lets her kids and their friends use cat food as a topping!"

Honestly, I don't know if Morgan's mom and dad allow their daughter to eat cat food. They might. They're more laid back than I am. Perhaps they're more sure of themselves. They seem less concerned with what others think of them than I do. I rationalize my fear by reasoning, *I'm a columnist. I'm a speaker. My husband works at American National Bank and is program chair for the Rockwall Noon Rotary. What would it do to us personally and professionally if it leaked out that our kids nibble kibble or munch Meow Mix when cravings rage?*

Molly interrupted my bout with social suicide.

"Do you want us to throw this away?"

Uh, *yeah!*

"Please do," I answered, counting to ten. Then, turning to Morgan, I said, "Sweetie, I don't know if your parents really allow you to eat cat food or not." Morgan nodded her head with vigor. "And I'm not sure I want to know," I went on, ignoring her silent insistence that Purina Cat Chow was one of her regular afternoon snacks and among her favorite munchies during Family Movie Night. "But when you're at our house, I just can't have you eating it. Do you understand?"

All three girls paraded to the trash can one by one to dump out perfectly good applesauce mixed with Meow Mix. As each plastic container hit bottom with a thump, they stared longingly, as though I'd made them toss out chocolate sundaes.

As I walked back to the bedroom, I was reminded of a longtime family friend. Grant heads up the risk management department for a large animal food conglomerate. He tours manufacturing plants all over the world, ensuring safety to keep the company's risk level as low as possible. Part of his job includes taste testing dog and cat food (dry and wet). He claims he's genuinely developed a liking for it. (Of course, I remember him eating shrimp still in the shells and the entire corncob when he was younger, so what does he know about taste—really?)

However, if Grant, who's a successful businessman and wine collector, can stomach cat food, maybe it's not so bad after all.

Another family friend, Drew, claims he survived on Purina Dog Chow and maple syrup during a two-day poker game in college.

Perhaps I'm the one who needs to open my mind and expand my horizons. Maybe instead of fighting 'em, I should join 'em.

Nah! I'll stick with people food, things I ate during pregnancy cravings and never stopped—like a bowl of cookie dough or olives pureed with Greek pepper juice.

Leslie Wilson's weekly humor column, "Reality Motherhood," entertains Dallas-area readers. She's also written for *Chicken Soup for the Mother of Preschooler's Soul, The Groovy Chicks' Road Trip* series, and dozens of parenting publications. She speaks to thousands each year at MOPS, ECPTAs, and Hearts at Home conferences. Visit www.RealityMotherhood.com.

3

Stuck in the Music

by Marla Ringger

I could tell something was wrong as soon as she got in the car. My normally happy-go-lucky eight-year-old pressed her lips tightly together as she slumped into the front seat, backpack still attached. No smile, no "Hi, Mom," no acknowledgements or waves to her friends. Just a quiet, defeated little girl.

It would have been so easy to just start the car, pretend everything was fine, and head for home. Instead, I started in. "Hi, Leslie. What's the matter?" "Nothing," she muttered. "Come on, honey...what happened? Did you get in trouble with the teacher?" "No." (Silence) "Did you have a fight with your friends?" "No." (Silence) "Did you get a bad grade?" "No." (Silence) "Well, what is it, then? Something happened...tell me," I said, trying gently to persuade her.

With her head down, Leslie peered up at me. "Promise you won't laugh?" I assured her I wouldn't. "Well, in music class, I was sitting by Micki, and I was holding the tambourine, and well, she dared me to put it over my head, and then, well, she dared me to put it around my waist, so I did. And it got stuck."

Astonished, I put my face in my hands and I laughed. Though I had promised her that I wouldn't, I simply couldn't help it. Leslie was the youngest of my three daughters, and I had never heard this one before. A tambourine stuck around a little girl's waist! I would not have imagined such a thing could even be possible.

Despite my laughter, Leslie continued with the story. It seemed that Micki was only half serious with her dare. In fact, she had turned away almost immediately after she spoke and was talking to a friend on the other side of her. Leslie, meanwhile, slipped the tambourine over her head and wormed around until it was lodged around her waist. She tapped Micki on the shoulder to show off her accomplishment. As Micki turned her head to look at her, she gasped in horror, incredulous that Leslie had taken her at her word.

Leslie was quite proud of herself...until she tried to wiggle out of it. As much as she wiggled, the tambourine would not budge past her shoulder blades. The harder she struggled, the more nervous she became. She was trying to do this without being noticed by the other kids. Unfortunately, her constant movement made the tambourine jingle, and soon everyone was aware of her problem. With all eyes on Leslie, she responded with, "What are you looking at?"

Things proceeded to get worse. Soon there was a group of eight little know-it-all third-grade girls who each wanted to offer a solution. To top it off, Leslie noticed the fifth graders peeking around the corner from the hallway, waiting to come in.

Finally, Mrs. Yahnig, the music teacher, took charge and told Leslie to wait in her office until she could help her. It took several painful yanks before she could get the tambourine to come off. (Mrs. Yahnig confided to me later that she thought she was going to have to call the custodian to cut the thing off!) Adding to her humiliation, Leslie then had to walk past the stares of the older kids to get back to her homeroom, only to deal with all the questions and exclamations from her own classmates.

So here I was, in the car with my little girl, trying to console her as best I could. I didn't say much. I offered her my arms and held her for a bit while she dried her eyes. In a town as small as ours, it wouldn't take long for this story to get around in more than one version. What could I say that would make any future remarks from well-meaning (and some not so well-meaning) friends less embarrassing? I could only offer her the assurance that one day she would laugh about this. And not only would she laugh about it, but she would want to tell it for the sheer pleasure of making others laugh about it. It would go down in her history as a classic childhood memory.

Someday she would laugh about it. But for now, we were both quite content to let the comfort of a mother's arms begin to heal the wounded spirit of an eight-year-old girl.

Marla lives with Gary, her husband of thirty years. After staying home to raise her three daughters, she has been blessed with two sons-in-law and seven grandchildren. She is now privileged to work alongside Gary at Life International, a ministry dedicated to helping orphans. Visit www.lifeintl.org.

4

Caution: Children at Play

By Jenn Doucette

In my premommy days, it never occurred to me to bolt our furniture to the walls. I even pooh-poohed the suggestion in earthquake prevention class. Then my husband and I had three children in four years. Translation: an 8.2 on the parental Richter scale. Thus the implementation of "Operation Homeland Security."

During the toddler trenches, my life was one big plastic obstacle course; we were the proud owners of six baby gates. This protective paraphernalia usually elicited a snicker from our guests. However, when they discovered the barred second-story windows accompanied by our sober expressions and scuff marks halfway up the wall, the snickers turned to gasps, only to be replaced by a respectful, "Wow."

In retrospect, the only person in the family who could open the kitchen cupboards was our daughter, Katie. By age two she made Houdini look wimpy. She could wiggle out of every restraining device on the market. And trust me, we tried every restraining device on the market. Gates never stopped her. They merely slowed her down. Keeping track of Katie in the morning was simply a matter of timing. We knew after we heard the first thump that she had jumped out of her crib. We had roughly 20 seconds until we heard the second thump, which signaled her successful escape over a childproof baby gate.

One morning my timing was off, and before I had a chance to intervene Katie had managed to open a "locked" kitchen cupboard and drink down half a bottle of Dawn dish detergent. I know it was half a bottle because, while I was on the phone with Poison Control (yet again), I witnessed the entire volume, in all its blue glory, vault out of her mouth onto our new carpet. "The human body is an amazing thing," the Poison Control expert informed me. Yep, pretty amazing.

What is also amazing is that our moms didn't possess handy restraining tools such as car seats and toilet lid locks. They had to rely on motherly instincts and quick reflexes, poor things. They were frontierswomen in the wilderness of childhood activity. And our dear grandmothers lived in the era of housewives in high heels. Now there's a reality television show even I could get addicted to—*Survivor III: Last Mom Standing.*

We've since gone through four years of preschool, a new chandelier (don't ask), and an entire set of cupboard locks. Grade school busyness has replaced baby busyness: skateboards, baseball practice, sleepovers, swimming lessons, and monkey bars. Our protective gear has grown more sophisticated as well: helmets, knee pads, elbow pads, shin guards, and training wheels. The gear may change, but the strategy remains the same—protect them from themselves!

In order to keep a small measure of control amid the chaos, I make lists. "To-do" lists, "Shopping" lists, "Chore" lists, and "Cruises I'd like to go on" lists. As a mother of three mini-Houdinis, I've compiled two other lists. One is titled, *"Now that I'm a mom, I have more…"* The other is, *"Now that I'm a mom, I have less…"* Not surprisingly, the "More" list is composed of items like stretch marks, bathtub toys, car seats, sippy cups, winter coats, Popsicle stick collections, and rubber snakes.

The "Less" list. Well, the Less list is fairly lengthy. And somewhat predictable: less sleep, free time, stomach muscle tone, uninterrupted adult conversation, and room in the hall closet for frivolous things, like snow skis and tennis rackets (see the "More" list under winter coats). The positive side of the More/Less lists so outweighs the negative. I have discovered as parents we have more bubble gum, giggling, tickling, ice cream, bubble baths, snow sledding and snowman making, more Chronicles of Narnia and Dr. Seuss, more pancakes and cereal for dinner, more pride. The good kind of pride. The kind of pride you experience when your child performs in her first school play, dressed like a pink firefly, of all things. More! More! More! And Less! Less mindless television, less stagnancy, less boredom, less selfishness.

As I watch my children mature, I find it difficult to remember having that much excitement for life. Too often I face each day with an attitude of mature mediocrity rather than childlike zip and zest. The daily grown-up tasks in my garden of responsibilities require an endless amount of watering, fertilizing, and trimming. I simply don't have time to smell the roses or swing from chandeliers. Or so I tell myself.

But then I think of my two lists.

Last September our youngest started kindergarten. Although the urge to pore over her baby book was great, I bravely appeased my nostalgia with a tall decaf vanilla latte and thoughts of the More/Less lists. I also addressed some serious housekeeping needs. The last outlet plugs and cupboard locks were removed, for convenience more than anything else. Remnants of the days of tiny baby fingers and big mom worries.

This year my kids are all in school, my house is cleaner, my cat is calmer, and my mind is clearer. Strangely enough, I kind of miss the scuff marks. Probably because those marks symbolize an existence bent on pursuing that which is just out of reach. Daily reminders to live life on the edge—or, more likely—life on the ledge.

You want to know the best parenting advice? Expect the unexpected. Wear a helmet. And eat your Wheaties. The extra carbs will help level the playing field between you and your rambunctious three-year-old.

Yes, my kids are busy. They are also intelligent, artistic, courageous, adventurous, and tenacious. Traits I so ardently desire. Perhaps this morning, after I wave goodbye to the school bus, I'll set aside some of my never-ending responsibilities and take a deep breath. Maybe I'll try a little wall climbing of my own. Our hallways are shockingly unspoiled by fresh paint; a few scuff marks might do us all a world of good. And besides, the furniture is bolted to the wall.

enn Doucette is mother and caregiver to three children, seven chickens, one hamster, one cat, and two fish named Gary and Larry. Her published works include *Mama Said There'd Be Days Like This* and *The Velveteen Mommy*. Jenn and Ben Doucette and family live in the Seattle area.

5

Happy "Balentine" Day Returns

by Jennifer Glewen

One day I remember fondly was last year's Valentine's Day, when I was eight months pregnant with our fourth son. I was having one of those days. You know the kind, where everything drives you crazy and nothing goes right? I was going to get some groceries with my three sons (seven, five, and two years old) when my husband called and said I should wait until he got home. He would watch the boys that evening so I could do my shopping. Well, I thought that was the sweetest thing because it's very rare that I get to go shopping by myself.

A few hours later my husband came home and took charge of our sons, just as he had promised. I thought, *This must be my Valentine's gift, a quiet shopping trip. How nice!* Boy, was I wrong.

My shopping trip was uneventful and I bought some things to put together a quick supper. I tried to hurry, hoping my husband wasn't getting too stressed by having the kids all alone. But to my surprise, he had everything under control and then some. What happened when I got home is something I will never forget.

As I pulled into the driveway I thought the house looked a little dark. *That's strange. Andy must have taken the boys somewhere.* I pulled into the garage, shut the car off, and got out to start unloading the groceries. With my arms full of bags, I walked to the door. As I started to open it I noticed that there was something taped to it, a home-made restaurant sign made by my seven-year-old. It said, Welcome to Glewen and Sons Restaurant.

At that moment, the door swung open and my middle son greeted me with a big smile. He had on a little tux and was holding his arm out for me to take. So of course I dropped the groceries!

"Welcome to Glewen and Sons Restaurant. May I seat you?" he asked. Talk about the cutest thing I have ever seen! And it kept getting better. As he led me into the candlelit kitchen, I could see my youngest son, also in a tux, holding a bouquet of flowers. He said, "Here, Mom. Happy Balentine's Day."

You can guess what happened next. That's right, I started weeping. My oldest son wasn't quite sure what to do. He had been instructed by my wonderful, loving husband to ask if I would like a salad; he wasn't expecting me to be crying like a baby. He thought I was going to be happy. After some reminding and encouraging from my husband, he got back on track and began serving me the most wonderful Valentine's dinner I have ever had.

I learned a little while later that my husband had orchestrated the entire evening with a "little" help from his mom. She made the tuxes that all the boys were wearing *and* prepared the entire meal, right down to beautifully decorated heart cookies.

I will never forget how special my family made me feel. Being a mom is an important job, and it feels so good when you are recognized for it. But it doesn't always have to be something as elaborate as a Valentine's dinner. Sometimes getting dandelions and little handmade notes is all you need to remember that you are valued and loved. God made me the mother of little boys for a reason: to love and care for them. They definitely returned that love one special Valentine's Day!

*J*ennifer Glewen is a 32-year-old stay-at-home mother of four boys, with a fifth boy on the way. She is an RN who works occasionally at a local hospital. She grew up, and still lives, in the Waupun, Wisconsin, area where she met her husband of 11 years.

6

Beads and Kryptonite

by Valerie Stranathan

If the fashion industry takes my advice, the "must have" gift for next Mother's Day will be a T-shirt imprinted with a large Superman logo. Of course, it will be done in pink, entwined with a rose, and bear the title "Supermom." With our various talents, skills, and experience, what mother among us doesn't deserve to be known as Supermom? I have converted a common red wagon into a prairie schooner and constructed Viking helmets out of construction paper. I even allowed my overly ambitious (and overly tall) three-year-old to ride the double loop roller coaster she'd been eying all day. The pride—and terror—shining out of her eyes when it was over was worth overcoming my own reservations about letting my three-year-old go flying upside-down through the air.

Alas, just like Superman, my powers of strength and bravery can be overcome by kryptonite. Of course, in my case it's spelled b-l-o-o-d and can really make a situation…interesting. Let me set the scene for you. I had allowed my two daughters to make a craft using small beads, and from the other room I heard Lydia start crying. I came in and found her scratching frantically at her nose. Great. "You put a bead up your nose, didn't you?" I asked. Nods and more incoherent blubbering sent me off to find a flashlight. I didn't see anything, but when the nose in question belongs to a wriggling, screaming contortionist, that doesn't mean much.

One phone call and two hours later, we were in the treatment room at the pediatrician's office. As we waited for the doctor, I looked around and found a drawer marked "Nose Suction." Hmm, it looks as though we aren't the only ones to make this trip.

The door opened and a doctor who looked exactly like Orville Redenbacher, down to the bow tie, walked in. I had to sheepishly admit that I had no idea which nostril was blocked; I wasn't even sure there *was* anything in there because Lydia had stopped crying an hour ago and seemed fine. The nurse held Lydia down while Dr. Redenbacher peered in her tiny nose. Nothing on the right side. Ah, there it was on the left. Whew! I wasn't just a paranoid, overreactive mother. It took two tools, a patient doctor, a very strong nurse, and me to hold her down and get the bead out.

Once the bead was out, a little blood appeared in her nose, not unexpected considering the tools the doctor had just used, but as we sat her up, the flood came. The nurse grabbed a handful of tissues and told me to hold them against her nose, hoping the pressure would stop the bleeding. We quickly soaked through the tissues and switched to paper towels. The doctor finished writing on the chart and left, and the nurse was in and out of the room, leaving me to deal with a thrashing, angry child who was fighting me while I tried to keep those towels pressed against her nose.

Now, I'm frequently called on to handle all kinds of difficult situations as a mom. From the unidentified gunk in the middle of the floor to the little sister who's trying to "help" with a game, Supermom is on the job. "Scary," "gross," and/or "smelly" don't phase me. When Kathryn spotted a snake beside the path at the zoo, we watched in fascination as it tried to climb a tree. I pointed out the difference between that one and the copperhead we watched a few weeks later cross the path at a nature center. I even killed a bee with my bare hands when it wouldn't leave Kathryn alone, impressing the heck out of the guy standing next to me. Hey, you don't mess with my kids.

But then the kryptonite comes in—Mama don't do blood. Please don't get me wrong. I've cleaned up my share of scrapes and cuts. I can wipe blood off a skinned knee and slap a Band-Aid on with the best of 'em, but if something bleeds more than a couple minutes, I'm toast. I've scared many a doctor, nurse, and lab technician by passing out whenever I have to give a blood sample. Or watch someone else give blood. Or just think about blood (hey, there's nothing wrong with a vivid imagination).

Lydia's nose continued to spout blood, and I was *not* handling it well. I was starting to get woozy, so I picked her up and moved to the chair with her in my lap. She was still screaming and fighting to get down, and I was fighting to stay upright. Finally, I asked Kathryn to get the nurse. Nurse Judy came back in and took one look at the situation, grabbed Lydia, and yelled for another nurse to take care of Mom. I ended up on the floor with my head between my knees and the nurse fanning away for dear life. Two patients for the price of one!

After an ice pack for the nose, a glass of water for Mom, and suckers for both girls, we were finally ready to leave the office. As we drove home, Kathryn, who was keeping a close eye on Lydia to make sure her nose didn't start gushing again, spoke up from the backseat. "I guess God answered my prayer," she said.

"Really?" I asked. "What did you pray for?"

"I prayed that Lydia's nose would stop bleeding and that you would be okay." Kathryn paused for a moment. "I also learned something for when I'm a mom. I'm going to tell my kids to never stick anything up their nose."

Good lesson! I also learned a valuable lesson. If this experience wasn't traumatic enough to keep Lydia from putting stuff up her nose, next time Dad would be taking her to the doctor!

*L*ife in the Stranathan household includes Valerie, her amazing husband, Will, their beautiful daughters Kathryn (seven) and Lydia (four), and Tinker the cat. Between homeschooling, housework, and managing everyone's schedules, it's a wild and wonderful circus, and she wouldn't change a thing.

Friend2Friend, Mom2Mom

7

The Fine Art of Self-Care

By Jill Savage

Mom, will you play ball with me? I need to work on my catching."
"Mom, can you wash my cross-country shirt? I have a meet
tonight." "Mom, can we go shopping today for a new pair of jeans?
I've outgrown all the ones in my closet." "Mom, I need you to help
me look through my catalog for classes for the fall semester. I have to
register online by tomorrow." "Mom, can you pick up the silk flowers
for my bridesmaids' bouquets today?"

Believe it or not, every one of those questions was posed to me by
each of my five children, ages 10 to 21, within a 30-minute period
one summer day. By the time question number five was tossed my
way, I wanted to scream, "There's not enough of me to go around!"
Okay, I'll be honest. It wasn't one of my holier moments. I believe I
did scream those words and a few more. Then I sent myself to my
room, calmed down, apologized to my children, and asked for their
forgiveness. And life continued on.

No matter whether you have one child or a dozen, there are times
when you feel sucked dry by their constant requests (read: demands)
on your life. You feel pulled in a hundred different directions and
overwhelmed with everyone's needs and wants. Add the needs of a
marriage to the mothering responsibilities, and you have a recipe for

feeling overwhelmed quite often. Like the television commercial of yesteryear, you long to declare, "Calgon, take me away!"

Over my 22 years of mothering, I've learned that much of my responsibility as a mom is sorting through the requests, demands, and needs of each member of my family. My job is similar to that of an emergency room triage nurse who has to evaluate the medical cases that come in and determine whose needs are the most critical and who can wait a little while longer, if needed. Unlike the nurse, however, I have the challenge of validating everyone's requests and helping them feel valued, even if they have to wait to have their needs met. It's a delicate dance of listening and communicating.

Oh, and amid evaluating all of the requests for my time and attention, I have to remember that I have needs too. Because there's no one representing me in the midst of all the craziness, and I'm often too distracted to consider myself in the mix, I end up trying to meet everyone's needs on an empty emotional fuel tank. This would be like trying to run a dozen errands around town in a car on empty. If you try such a silly thing, you'll wind up on the side of the road with only half of your errands accomplished. Yet I often try to run relational errands on an empty emotional fuel tank. When I try such a silly thing, I'm destined for down time on the side of the road, and it's likely that no one's needs will be adequately met.

Learning the fine art of self-care has been a lifelong lesson for me. Self-care requires me to learn to think of me in a healthy, balanced way. It's different than being selfish or self-centered where I'm doing what I want to do for me and only me. Rather, self-care is the intentional filling of my emotional fuel tank to prepare me for meeting the needs of my family. Similar to filling up the fuel tank before taking a long car trip, self-care looks ahead to the goal and does the preparation to make sure you arrive at your destination.

I've also learned another lesson in the midst of the chaos: talking with God makes a big difference. The Bible talks about having peace that passes understanding (Philippians 4:7). On some of my more victorious mothering moments, that peace has carried me through what could only be described as pandemonium. I remember one time when

I had just changed the baby's diaper, put on fresh clothes after a diaper blowout, and wiggled his little body into a snowsuit to prepare him for a ride across town to drop his three older siblings off at school with a quick stop at the grocery store afterward. As soon as the snowsuit zipper met up with his pudgy little neck, I heard the sound again. It was another diaper blowout. Upon exploration, I determined this was worse than the first and it was going to require a bath, fresh clothes, and even another snowsuit. I didn't lose it though. I did what I had to. When one of the older kids came in to find out why the baby and I were taking so long to get in the car, I answered patiently that we'd had an unexpected delay. Then another sibling came in announcing that she'd forgotten her gym shoes and she didn't know where they were. Sibling number three ran in the house to find a permission slip he'd forgotten. It was complete chaos and yet, this time, I remained calm with a peace that certainly passed all understanding of what was happening around me. My little visits with God (reading a Bible verse while sitting for a brief minute by myself in the bathroom or praying while I was folding laundry) brought about a peace that defied the lunacy of the moment.

In the everyday challenges of mothering, chaos is inevitable. I will feel pulled apart piece by piece. The needs of my family will make up my to-do list. My perfect plans will be hijacked by the children I love. I'll be disappointed, overwhelmed, and stretched as thin as Silly Putty. But in the midst of it all, I have the opportunity to learn more about myself, my own needs, and most important, my need for a Savior who can get me through anything.

*J*ill Savage is the founder and executive director of Hearts at Home. She is the author of four books, including *Professionalizing Motherhood,* and the coauthor of *Got Teens?* Her most recent book, *My Heart's at Home,* looks at all the roles that home plays in our family's life. Jill is a pastor's wife and mother of five. She and her family make their home in Normal, Illinois. For more information visit her website: www.jillsavage.org.

8

Martha Mentor

By Donna Otto

A s a young mom I prayed for a mentor. You know, a righteous woman who would swoop in and praise my mothering, grant me insights and wisdom about life, and generally like me. A lot. She would be a mature but fashionable woman with a perfect family, poise, and confidence equal to her passion for God. This noble woman would be a pillar of the church, and, best of all, she would choose to mentor me. Seemed reasonable. After all, I believe in the power of prayer! Maybe Elisabeth Elliot could make house calls.

Of course, God granted this prayer. The part about the righteous woman, anyway. And what a blessing she was. Only God did it His way, not mine, and I am so glad He did. Otherwise, I might never have come to know and love Martha.

Martha was not Elisabeth Elliot. She was a local lady in the church with four (later five) daughters of her own and a hardworking older husband. She was ten years older than I was, and she saw something in me that needed mending and tending. She became my friend and mentor.

I wanted high fashion; Martha came from rural Arkansas where chickens ran wild in the front yard. I wanted poise and confidence;

Martha had a nervous laugh whenever anyone asked her to speak or do anything that might draw attention to her. I wanted to be a writer; Martha, although studious, was very shy, and the only writing she did was letters to relatives back home and cards of encouragement to me.

But Martha knew how to love. She loved God, her husband, her children, and the church. She even came to love me and my family. She could cook wondrous things in her cluttered kitchen. She taught me that love can be expressed by serving the ones God gives you. She managed a busy home with tons of laundry stacked in the oddest places. She taught me that people are more valuable than things, and life is lived every day in fresh new ways. Her daughters ran her ragged, but she never complained. She was an optimist when money was short and problems loomed large, which happened often. Her furniture was what we call "eclectic," meaning lots of castoffs that didn't always match, but her house had warmth and even style. She was a woman of faith and she modeled it for me. She let me into her life.

More than that, she helped me grow. With a word or phrase, usually delivered amid some task we were doing, Martha would cause me to think about key things in life and with my walk with the Lord. "How are you doing with your prayer life?" she would say as I was folding socks. Well, how did she know that I had let that little part of my walk slip? "What do you think God wants for your daughter?" she would ask. God wants something for my daughter? I would spend days pondering Martha's questions, and usually they led me back to the Bible and prayer. We would talk and talk about these questions, and I came to trust her and to learn. She had a wisdom that came from a long walk with a faithful God and knowledge of Scripture. Martha wasn't educated, but she was smart. More than that, she was wise.

She asked questions, not knowing the answers. She simply wanted God's best for me, and she was wise enough to know that if I grew close to Him, I was more likely to get His best. The rest of the many things I learned from my esteemed mentor came from watching her. Watching her humility and faith. Watching how she fried chicken.

Watching how she dealt with financial setbacks. Watching how she mothered a bunch of daughters, managed a household, sang in the choir, and encouraged a quiet husband. I even watched her find joy in a pregnancy at 45 years old. Another daughter.

And we laughed. Life is fun and funny when you have a Martha around. She would laugh at herself, which reminded me that life is not so serious after all. We would laugh at the predicaments I got myself into, because I have a gift for action and motion, not to mention commotion. Some of my best stories come from times with Martha and our families.

I remember the day when money was short at our house, really short, and Martha somehow knew it. She invited us for dinner. For three days we ate with Martha's family. Lots of home cooked food with enormous amounts of love and laughter. Ten people around the table. After dinner I did the dishes and Martha dried. We prayed as we worked. The stress of money troubles melted in the face of God's family. And sure enough, we made it through.

Martha and her husband are retired now; their children grown and gone. After 30 years we still connect and laugh together, although we are thousands of miles apart. I still get cards of encouragement. She is still a righteous woman, giving herself away.

And, do you know, in God's providence, I did actually get to meet and know Elisabeth Elliot. She was exactly the woman I had first dreamed of as a mentor! She ministered to me as well in a deep, wondrous, personal way. But there was only one Martha.

May God grant you a Martha.

*D*onna Otto is a noted speaker and author with a ministry to women, particularly mothers who choose to stay at home. She has been a frequent guest and speaker for Hearts at Home. Her most recent book is *Finding Your Purpose as a Mom*.

9

Pity Party

By Robyn Whitlock

My head hits the pillow and I feel the ache of too-little sleep as my body literally collapses. In the recesses of my brain, I begin to process that a baby is crying and wake with a start—I have a baby. I have two babies. And someone needs me.

I stumble into the nursery and pick up my wailing six-month-old, Andrew, while his twin brother, Bryce, snoozes on. A glance at the clock tells me it's morning, but my body rebels. Up and down all night, my twins "tag teamed" me, leaving me exhausted.

In the kitchen I hit the button on the coffeemaker and quickly heat a bottle for the hungry baby in my arms. My eyes fill with tears—motherhood is nothing like I thought it would be. Before kids I imagined an efficiently run home, happy children spaced at least three years apart, and a romantic partnership with my husband. The reality is basket after basket of laundry stacked in the dining room—both clean and dirty—twin boys who each want my undivided attention, and a husband who is wonderful, but in order to support us needs to travel constantly for work.

Balancing baby, bottle, and a coffee mug, I settle onto the couch for a pity party. Just as Andrew snuggles in with his bottle, I hear

Bryce crying upstairs. I listen for a few minutes while Andrew takes a few more gulps, and then I put him in his bouncy seat. He screams while I race upstairs. Soon an unhappy Bryce joins Andrew. Now I have two screaming babies to deal with and still only one of me. As I finish feeding Andrew, I sing to Bryce and rock his bouncy seat with my foot. "Hush now, Bryce. Mommy is doing her best." I wish I had never read in those twin books about tandem feeding because it wouldn't work for us. Born eight weeks premature, I needed to watch them closely while they ate to make sure they kept their suck, swallow, and breathe pattern steady. Listening to Bryce scream, I feel like a failure as a mom. There just isn't enough of me to go around.

The phone interrupts these thoughts, and I pick it up as I switch babies. With Andrew fed and happy in his bouncy seat, Bryce settles down with the bottle in his mouth.

"Hello?"

"Hi! It's Ellen," her chipper voice calls out. "How's it going?"

"Horrible," I confess. I'm feeling guilty as I cry. "I hate this. I can't do this."

"Oh, sweetie, yes, you can. Why don't you bring the babies over? I got a case of rice cereal in yesterday and I'm ready to divide it up!" Ellen, an eternal optimist, has triplets the same age as my boys and is always getting us a group discount on something.

"Ellen, I can't. I don't think I'll even leave the couch today, much less the house. Paul is gone, and I just can't cope. I gotta go."

Hanging up, I feel guilty for complaining to my friend. She has three babies, and she never complains! I put Bryce up on my shoulder to burp and feel the warm spit-up slide down my neck. Yuck. After changing myself and both boys, I stick my now cold coffee in the microwave just as the doorbell rings.

"Who could that be?" I ask the boys as I brush my fingers through my hair and swing the door open. It's Ellen. And her three babies. My face reddens as I invite her in. Had I really said that "it's too hard" to get out with my two babies? Now here she is with her three!

"You sounded like you could really use a friend," she explained as she put the box of rice cereal on the floor.

The tears fall freely now. I feel stronger for my tears. This is not too hard. I am the mother of two precious babies, and I am capable of taking care of them. I have to be. I'm the only mother they have.

Nothing really changed that day. My babies still get up in the middle of the night. They still need to be fed one at a time, and I'm convinced there will never be enough of me. But when I am tempted to complain, all I have to do is think of Ellen and her triplets, and I bite my tongue. I can do this too.

Robyn Whitlock lives in Naperville, Illinois, and has been married to her best friend, Paul, for ten years. She is the mother of three boys, Bryce, Andrew, and Benjamin. When she's not chasing after the boys, doing laundry, or running to carpool, she writes.

10

A Hand to Help

by Joy Kaurin

On Tuesday Brenna was absolutely miserable. I had been trying to wait out a cold with her, just positive that tomorrow she would feel better. Days later, she had a high fever, was lethargic, and refused to eat or drink. My husband was at class, neighbors were gone, friends were busy, and I realized I needed to take her to the doctor immediately.

I loaded my three young children up in the van and headed out to the hospital. Just outside the city limits, I began to question how to get the kids into the hospital with minimal exposure to the cold and questioned whether or not to take advantage of the free valet parking. I had seen the signs and the kind gentleman who waits by the main entrance, but somehow I didn't think I qualified as the sort who needed that help. *Oh, no,* I reasoned. *I'll just park up close and walk.*

The morning went downhill from there. Brenna was not happy to be at the medical center and refused to stay in the exam room. Sam added a few notes to Brenna's chart while I chased Brenna down the hall. I finally corralled Brenna back in the small room and held the children's attention with tongue depressors, latex gloves, and Dora stickers until the nurse came to see my daughter. We were soon thankfully clutching the prescription and making our way to the elevator when Brenna decided that she did like the medical center after all and wasn't ready to go quite yet. She promptly laid facedown on the floor and went limp.

Something in me snapped. I hoisted her up in one arm and shoved the stroller forward. It lurched and refused to move. Sam put his right thumb in his mouth for luck and gripped the front bar of the stroller with his left hand for safety while Emily watched with wide eyes. I lifted up the brake lock and heaved the stroller forward into the elevator, where a couple leaped apart and into separate corners for safety.

We rode down to the first floor in silence and allowed the innocent bystanders to exit first. As we stood in the elevator, I reminded Brenna of what she needed to do. "Brenna, you need to cooperate with Mommy. You need to hold Mommy's hand and help push the stroller." Eight feet from the elevator she went limp again and laid facedown on the floor.

I sighed loudly in frustration and stood next to her. I was past embarrassment at the stares, past caring if I would hurt her arm if I were to yank her up off of the ground, and definitely past my limit. I had passed up free valet parking and was now dealing with a four-year-old lying prone in the foyer at the medical center.

Just then a tiny woman walked up to me. "Can I please help you?" she said. "Um, sure…yeah," I said, stumbling over my words. "Yes, thank you. That would be great." I stood for a moment in silence. I didn't even know what to ask her to do to help. She automatically walked up to the stroller and introduced herself as I picked up my daughter, and then walked out to the parking lot. Her son was in the hospital for testing that day, she said, and she had had three stair-step children herself years ago. Oh, she sighed with a smile, she could remember what it was like. She pushed the stroller to the van so that I could load the children, and when I turned around, she was gone. I scanned the parking lot, looking to see where she had parked, but she was back up at the entrance, reentering the hospital.

As I drove home that morning it occurred to me that we are given opportunities to serve each other. Yet somehow it is so much easier to give a hand then accept extra help. This season of life is going to give me a new sense of awareness in helping others. I'd like to think that someday I might see a woman struggling with small children and ask with a smile, "Can I please help you?" My turn is coming.

*J*oy is a speaker, freelance writer, and, most important, wife to Greg and mother to Brenna, Sam, and Emily. Joy loves sharing about the challenges and rewards from parenting a child with special needs. She enjoys living in the Midwest and spending time with her family outdoors.

11

Moving Finds

by Patty Maier

My husband, Marcus, grew up on a farm in Central Illinois. He always dreamed of living on the farm again someday, and he shared that dream with me while we were dating. I had always lived in cities, but I told him that living in the country would be okay with me. (I was in love.)

We eventually settled in a small town nestled halfway between the family farm and the city where Marcus and I worked. Three years later our first child, Heidi, arrived, and I became a stay-at-home mom. All of a sudden, I needed "mom friends"—friends who had been there before me, and friends who were going through the same things I was going through. I had never needed girlfriends as much as I did then. Thank goodness I found some where we lived.

As soon as Heidi could talk, she started praying for "baby brother, baby sister" every night at bedtime. When Heidi was almost four, Ben and Gretchen were born. Our family was complete. We were acquainted with almost everyone in our small town. It was great knowing the children my kids were in school and preschool with, as well as their parents, teachers, and faculty. We had good neighbors and many friends, and we were very involved with church, social activities, and supporting our community.

Yet Marcus still longed to live on the family farm. I couldn't imagine living anywhere besides the small town that had become our home. I especially couldn't imagine living out in the country. I kept telling Marcus that I liked having neighbors. Marcus would always respond, "How do you know that you won't like *not* having neighbors?"

I wanted to keep the promise I'd made to Marcus before we got married, so I finally said we could move to the farm once all three children were in elementary school. But as that time drew near, I was dreading it. I was especially concerned about Heidi, my introverted daughter, having to change schools as she was going into fourth grade. So I started praying for her to have a new friend when we moved. I started praying the same thing for myself. I prayed and prayed.

I drove the kids to school on their first day at the new school. We knew no one there. A friend told me she had a friend who lived in the same school district as us. She said her friend had a daughter named Erin who was Heidi's age. I was anxious for Heidi to get home so I could ask her if she'd met Erin.

When Heidi got off the bus after school that day, she exclaimed, "Mom, I made a new friend! Her name is Erin." I couldn't believe it. What are the odds? But I had prayed, so I shouldn't have been surprised. It filled me with hope. I was still looking for the new friend for me that I'd prayed for. God didn't answer my prayer in the way I expected, though.

Before we were able to move, we had to gut most of the farmhouse. For nine months we worked hard getting the house ready for our family. During that time, some of my friends pulled away. Others were busy with their own lives, while I was busy with mine. I started talking more and more to someone I'd never been close to before. Her name was Jill. It wasn't that our paths didn't cross before then. On the contrary, her oldest daughter was our favorite babysitter, her middle daughter was in my Girl Scout troop with Heidi, and her youngest daughter was in preschool with my younger two children.

Jill and I were on our MOPS (Mothers of Preschoolers) steering team together. Our children swam on the same swim team. We ran in the same circles, but we'd never really connected...until my family started the process of moving.

When I prayed for a new friend, I was expecting the friend to be in our new community, not in our old town 23 miles away. I never expected that friend to be Jill. But God knows what's best. His timing is perfect. Jill and I aren't in the same circles anymore, but Jill is still a mom like me. She is one of my closest friends. We share and encourage each other through e-mail, talk when we can, pray for each other, and get together for lunch as our schedules permit.

As for Heidi, she and Erin didn't become close friends. But when we found a new church home, Heidi found a new best friend named Anna. Because of their friendship, Anna's brother Nik has become friends with my son Ben, and Anna's mom, Traci, and I have become good friends. Our husbands have even gone to the races together. God is good.

Yesterday was the first day of school again. Heidi is now in sixth grade. She came home from school saying she'd made a new friend with someone who's new to the school. This morning when the school bus pulled up, I saw that little girl in the window. She had a huge smile on her face because she was excited to see Heidi. I couldn't help but wonder if Heidi is the friend that little girl's mom prayed for.

*P*atty is wife to Marcus and mom to Heidi, Ben, and Gretchen. Along with being a stay-at-home mom, Patty enjoys reading, writing, editing, and encouraging others. She is the director of the *Hearts at Home* magazine. Before becoming a mother, Patty was a computer systems analyst.

12

Change of Heart

By Gina Frandle

With a fresh, beautiful baby boy lying on my lap, I sat crying in the bathroom waiting for him to stop his howling cries as he waited for something I had no idea how to give him. I had shut myself away in the bathroom because the house was full of people welcoming a growing family home. My mind was spinning in directions I had no control over. As I looked down at Eythan, his fingers curled into tight little fighting fists, knuckles white, mouth wide open apparently sharing with me his need, tears drenched the front of my shirt. "God help me" was my cry. He was so much easier to take care of in the womb. I didn't have to clothe him or change diapers. I even remember wanting to be pregnant again...maybe even step back across time during our amazing honeymoon and take more precaution and start our family a little later in our marriage. Eythan was beautiful, but my heart wasn't.

My husband, David, had plans for children in our marriage. I, on the other hand, had absolutely no desire for kids. As a teenager I would be asked to babysit neighbor kids and I would find ways of saying no. The only reason I ever said yes was when I needed money. Kids were pests. They were rude, had no control over their bowels, and worse yet, they needed a great deal of attention. I had organized plans for myself, and those plans didn't involve children. I was to go to college, get my degree, and work in television broadcasting in New York. You see, there it was. My plan. It was infallible and complete. It had no deviations concerning kids. I supposed I would marry one day, but that was even in the distant future. Then I fell in love with David, a strong yet gentle man who carried with him a love for his Savior, Jesus. When I unwrapped his personality I found the puzzle piece the Lord had placed right in front of me for a husband. We married in June and my doctor told me the news of my pregnancy in August. How could I have let a "mistake" like this happen?

As my puffy red eyes, wet with tears, fell back on the squirming newborn in my arms, I heard a light knock on the bathroom door and a pleading voice asking me, "Is everything all right?" Bringing me out of my pity party, I gave a squeaky response. "No." My mom slowly opened the door, her eyes met mine, and her mother's heart knew I needed her. Oh, how I treasure that moment now. She knelt beside me as I sat occupying the only "chair" in the bathroom and prayed a prayer only she and I knew I needed. It wasn't an oratory; it was simple and to the point. She closed her eyes, touched my shoulder and placed her hand on Eythan, and helped me cleanse my heart and bring peace to my home. She prayed, "Lord, give my daughter a mother's heart."

It has been 16 years since that emotional day in the bathroom. The Lord answered my mom's heartfelt prayer in an amazing way. As only God could, He changed my stiff heart to that of a loving mother's heart. I not only love and cherish my three kids, but I also enjoy many young friendships as well as teach third-grade Sunday school.

Thank You, Lord, for listening to the cry of a mother who loved her daughter and a daughter who didn't have any desire to be a mother 16 years ago.

*G*ina Frandle grew up in southern Minnesota where she, along with her husband, David, are raising and home-schooling their children; Eythan—16, Ashlen—14, and Morgan—12. After 22 years in Christian radio, she now takes excitement in being a full-time mom, speaking, writing, graphic design, and gardening.

The Art of Everyday Mothering

13

Mount Guiltmore

by Julie Ann Barnhill

My children have an impatient, quirky, hardworking, verbose, affectionate, opinionated, forgiving, occasionally cranky, and ever-so-slightly neurotic mom who loves them madly. A neurotic mother who over the gamut of her mothering experience (17 years, 5 months, 28 days, 7 hours, 17 minutes, and 16 seconds) has often belabored the minutiae of mothering life. Trust me—no trivial detail has escaped the proclivities of my maternal angst.

It officially started in January 1988 as I pored over pregnancy and medical reference books, hoping to discern if the formation of my first child had in any manner been compromised due to my consuming celebratory glasses (yes, *plural*) of Asti Spumante approximately six hours prior to her, um…rather unexpected conception. (We shall always consider Kristen to be our honeymoon souvenir gift.)

A few weeks afterward (it seems), I was slathering coconut butter on my ever-expanding belly and courageously attempting to swallow prenatal vitamins roughly the size of a man's big toe each morning before eating breakfast and leaving for work.

I was absolutely determined to do everything right with my pregnancy and as a mother.

That's when I began the first of many conversations with my baby when she approximated the size and shape of a small lima bean. An article in *Perfect Mother* magazine had convinced me that any hope of a successful nurturing of the mother-child bond depended on the baby's ability to hear and recognize my voice. Hence my daily conversational ramblings.

I talked and talked and talked. Actually, I haven't stopped talking since.

And she was an excellent listener—back then.

Yes, I was determined to do everything right. I cut back—way back—on my daily consumption of Pepsi, refused to walk (or breathe) within a 100-yard radius of a cat litter box, and carefully measured the width between slats before settling on a beautiful *safe* cherry wood crib. In addition, having read *The Womanly Art of Breastfeeding*, I began "preparing" those womanly mammary glands for active duty. (It involved sandpaper and sure-grip pliers—we'll leave it at that.)

I read other books as well. Magazines too—a lot of them. Over the course of nine months I purchased, borrowed, and inhaled reams of written material. What information I couldn't find there, I asked of other mothers.

Was it normal for hair to grow exponentially on one's belly while pregnant?

Could the baby sense when I was worried, fearful, or enjoying sex? (The possibility of the latter *really* freaked me out.)

Should I have a water birth, sit on a birthing stool, or strap my legs into stirrups?

Was it bad to want as many pain-numbing drugs as possible— during the seventh month of pregnancy?

Would the fact that I never qualified for National Honor Society hold my child back intellectually?

In light of said academic reality, should I purchase the *Baby Einstein* encyclopedia set with annotated appendixes for the low cost of $15,397.22—a mere $6.89 less than my entire teaching salary for the year, but sure to guarantee that lima bean baby would qualify for the ranks of Mensa?

Were ankles roughly the size of Babar the Elephant's a positive or negative indicator regarding pregnancy weight gain?

And how would I ever be able to determine when I was in real labor? (Okay, I was both slightly neurotic and altogether clueless!)

I had the minutiae of anticipatory maternal neuroses down to a science. By the second trimester I had considered (obsessed over) the following:

Would I be able to interpret my baby's cries?

Would I bump her head into the doorknob while carrying her in my arms?

Would my milk come in?

And more troublesome still—upon careful examination and comparison of two-dimensional breast-feeding diagrams with actual breasts (mine)—how on earth were my now monstrous-sized mammary attachments going to fit within the minuscule circumference of a newborn baby's mouth?

These were the things that kept me up at night! As well as the even more basic worries that haunted me throughout those early months.

What if my baby didn't like me?

What if I didn't like her?

What if I did it all wrong?

And that, of course, was just the beginning. It was my first glimpse of the mountainous terrain that looms over every mother's life. My first view of the familiar and foreboding range of peaks I've come to call Guiltmore National Park.

You won't be able to locate Guiltmore on a Rand McNally travel atlas. Nor will a list of websites appear after you enter certain key words in Google. But it's there—this mountainous range of regret, second-guessing, and doubt that can only be seen, observed, trekked, and experienced from a mother's backyard.

It's a familiar sight where most of us live. And it still looms for me, even though my lima bean baby is now closing in on adulthood with her brothers close behind her. And many days I still find myself trekking the rocky slopes of Guiltmore, pondering questions that range from the mundane to momentous:

Was this cavity the result of too many juice boxes when he was little?

Should we have let her quit piano?

Did all our moves make our children flighty and insecure?

If I let them sleep late this summer morning (so I can get some writing done), will they grow up to be lazy slugs?

You see, for nearly two decades—ever since those lima bean days—I have awoken to equal parts mothering mayhem and mothering bliss. And a day hasn't gone by in which something wasn't said, done, thought, forgotten, screamed, denied, or remembered and held hostage by guilt.

Not one day.

Yes, guilt will always be part of the mothering landscape.

But pay attention because this is important: It doesn't have to *dominate* your landscape. It doesn't have to ruin your life, spoil your fun, or rob you of peace of mind.

Motherhood may be a dependable source of guilt—and it seems to be mandatory for every mom to spend some time hiking on Guiltmore.

At the same time, God uses the experience of motherhood to provide us with a steady supply of what we need to leave Guiltmore in the distance and keep on moving lightly down the road.[1]

Julie Ann Barnhill's hilarious yet thought-provoking speaking and writing resonate with thousands of listeners and readers. Interviewed by Oprah Winfrey and Dr. James Dobson, Julie has also written the bestseller *She's Gonna Blow!* as well as the Hearts at Home book *Motherhood: The Guilt That Keeps On Giving.* Julie and her husband, Rick, live in Illinois with their three children.

14

I Love Smelly Shoes

by Lysa TerKeurst

The art of thanksgiving is one we should all pass on to our children. I'm not talking about the holiday with pumpkin pie and turkey. I'm not talking about decorating with cornucopias, dried corn stalks, and scarecrows. I'm not talking about setting a candlelit table with fancy linens and fine silver. While those are all artistic ways of expressing the day of Thanksgiving, I'm talking about the attitude of thankfulness that can so easily get looked over. I'm talking about the art of saying *thank you* in the everyday.

I am so blessed. But I'm also guilty of becoming so distracted by my blessings that I forget to thank the One from whose hands these things come. Do I see the loving husband I've been blessed with, or do I just grumble about his faults? Do I see the creative child I am blessed with, or do I just grumble about her artistic messes? Do I see the health of a son who can play sports as a blessing, or do I just grumble about the sweaty laundry? Do I see the home I am blessed to have, or do I just grumble about the constant chores to keep it clean? Do I see how blessed we are to have food whenever we want, or do I just grumble about a kitchen that never seems to stay clean? You get the picture.

I decided I wanted to get more intentional with expressing my thankfulness. I also wanted to get more intentional with developing an attitude of thankfulness in my children. I want the words *Thank you* to fall so easily from their lips that it becomes second nature. Without thinking or much effort, they say thank you for both the big and small. I want them to say it to the Lord, people they know, and even those they don't know but should express gratitude to.

Realizing I must model what I teach, I decided to assess how thankful I really am. As I made a mental list of those things I was thankful for, I suddenly became distracted with the unusual amount of out-of-place shoes scattered about my home. Not so spiritual, I know. But the shoes seemed to be coming out of the woodwork and screaming for my attention. I went from having a full heart focused on God to a grumbling woman suddenly feeling frustrated and drained. How many times have I picked up shoes? In my motherhood journey, how many shoes will I pick up and put back, only to pick them up and put them back again…and again…and again?

I counted 14 pairs of shoes that were just within eyesight of where I was sitting. Upon further inspection, they were everywhere—by the back door, the front door, in the laundry room, in the hallway, in the kitchen, by the dog dish, on the stairs, in the guest bathroom, in my bathroom, on the floor in the kids' bedrooms and even in the linen closet. I was frustrated that these shoes weren't where they were supposed to be. Visions of chore charts and consequences for leaving your things out and about started dancing in my mind. I even went so far as to think that this was yet more evidence that my kids are not as thankful as they should be. Kids who were truly thankful for their shoes would care enough to tuck them into their closet shoe racks.

But as I mentally chided my children for their ungratefulness, I felt God gently give me a piece of my own reprimand. Was I modeling thankfulness in this moment? Was I exemplifying what I had on my heart to make sure my kids modeled in their everyday life? Scattered shoes are a normal, everyday thing with a hidden treasure about them. It's all in how I choose to look at these shoes that will determine whether I feel drained and frustrated or filled up and thankful.

I stopped and thanked God for this evidence of life. Some had grass and dirt on them as proof that our kids were healthy and strong enough to run and play. Some had scuff marks from one too many dances on the concrete outside. Some had teeth marks from our beloved dog, Champ, who's favorite pasttime is chasing kids, balls, and stray shoes. One had paint on it from a school project. But all were well worn, broken in, and definitely used.

So, here I am walking in this season of my life's journey with soccer cleats, princess shoes, basketball high-tops, teenager want-to-be boots, kitten bedroom slippers, and gymnastics flip-flops. Funny how these shoes tell stories of life, if only I make the choice to listen. Games won and lost, girlhood fantasies, dreams of the future, comforts of home, and expressions of style.

Maybe you've felt a little frustrated with the shoes scattered about your home as well. But the next time you pick them up, instead of letting frustration whisk you away, listen carefully to the story they tell. Listen carefully and thank God for each and every evidence of life.

I put the shoes in a big pile in the middle of my kitchen and took a picture. They weren't neatly arranged and perfectly matched. Oh, no. They were just scattered and tossed about. It looked like a little shoe party and all sizes and shapes were invited. I think I'll frame this picture and let it remind me often of the beauty of a refueled approach.

It's all in how I look at things that makes a world of difference. If my approach is one that living life simply drains me, then I'll constantly feel drained. But if I can pull back the veil and peek behind the messes, chores, and faults of others, I'll see the treasure of what these things represent. I'm a wife! I'm a mom! I've been handed the privilege to fulfill these eternally significant roles for some pretty amazing people...my family!

So, what about my thankful list? I eventually got back to that. I'm thankful for the gift of our Savior. I am thankful for my husband and kids. I am thankful for friends and extended family. I am thankful for our home full of life and lots of activity. And, strangely enough, I'm really thankful for shoes...especially the smelly ones![2]

*L*ysa TerKeurst is a wife to Art and mom to five priority blessings named Jackson, Mark, Hope, Ashley, and Brooke. She is the author of 11 books with her latest release being *What Happens When Women Say Yes to God*. Her greatest passion is inspiring women to say yes to God and take part in the awesome adventure He has designed every soul to live. While she is the cofounder of Proverbs 31 Ministries, to those who know her best she is simply a carpooling mom who loves her family, loves Jesus passionately, and struggles like the rest of us with laundry, junk drawers, and cellulite.

15

Mom's Day In

by Sherry McCaulley Palmer

I am writing this in the closet. Well, part of it, anyway. It's Mother's Day, and...um...the fact is, I'm locked in the closet. I have nowhere to go, so I have grabbed the nearest shoebox lid and the pen in my pocket, and decided I might as well seize the moment. The closet door in our upstairs bedroom sticks and is next to impossible to budge when it's closed, so we never close it completely. Until today, that is. For weeks now I have been trying to teach my child how to shut the door without breaking the sound barrier. When he is in a hurry, whatever door he's going out of typically gets slammed behind him, and he has not yet grasped my personal open door policy. *If you can't shut it quietly, then leave it open.*

What is it about doors that makes us want to slam them? Sometimes we slam doors because you can get your point across without ever opening your mouth. It's like saying *"There! Take that!"* With one yank of the door handle, pictures on the wall are reassembled and the shelves becomes sliding boards for knickknacks, some of which crash onto the floor to be quickly intercepted by the puppy. What was once a treasured item becomes pounced and shredded, all with the slamming of a single door. Therefore, in our house the shelf which once contained memorabilia now displays doggie yummies and chew sticks. At least that way when the door gets slammed, the dog gets fed.

Personally, I don't like slamming doors. Especially when my face is in the way. Still, if the door has to be slammed, I must admit that I would rather be the slammer, not the slammee.

Lately when "O ye of little feet" slams the door, I have required that he retrace his steps and demonstrate that he knows how to shut the door quietly. Unfortunately, today he once again forgot the basic steps involved in Door Shutting 101, when he followed me into the closet, promptly slamming the door behind him. The problem was, the door he slammed happened to be the one that sticks. And since it takes King Kong to open it, I've had a no-holds-barred, three-alarm Mom's Day In.

We had just returned home from church and I had lunch on the brain. Wanting to fully appreciate the occasion, I had gone upstairs to change into something more comfortable.

Slam. It could only mean one thing; we were in here, lunch was out there. Not good. In a panic I switched on the light, grabbed the door handle and yanked it several times. No luck. Next I slammed my rotund body against the door. Surely that would jar it loose. Fat chance.

"Help!" I screamed. No response. I proceeded to beat on the door with my fists and screamed again. And again. I jumped up and down on the floor. My child joined in. "Daddy, Daddy!"

"Have faith," I said. "Daddy will hear us."

What was I thinking? This is a huge old farmhouse and no one was going to hear us. Why? Because someone I know and love had assumed the position on the couch in front of the television. What was that my hubby had mentioned about resting his eyes for a few minutes? I turned to my son. "If you hadn't slammed the door, this would not have happened," I scolded. Even he didn't hear me. Why? Because he had stuck his fingers in his ears.

Suddenly my thoughts turned from "Where is lunch?" to "When will we get out of here?" I looked around the floor, assembled a sort of padding, sat my rump down, and hoped that a spider would not crawl out at me. "Oh, why don't they put Port-a-Potties in closets?" I asked my son. Actually, it does not take much gray matter between the ears to figure this one out; it's because they don't fit, that's why. There's simply no space for a Port-a-Potty when the closet is already occupied by two human beings, blankets, extra pillows, junk I shoved in there before our last open house, magazines I had intended to throw away, suitcases, hats no one will ever wear, clothes that no longer fit but are being kept in storage just in case, old shoes, a bathing suit that could frighten mice, a wasp clinging to the light bulb, extension cords, coats, scarves, gloves, and who knows what else. Why hadn't I used this closet to store emergency food, a dorm-sized refrigerator, and a stove?

One hour passed. We hollered for help. Two hours passed. We hollered and jumped. Three hours passed with apparently no rescue in sight, so we sat down, sang every song we knew, and then finally fell asleep. At last we woke to the sound of my husband's voice.

"Honey, time for lunch," I heard the object of my affections calling from the kitchen. What? I'm not missed unless someone's stomach is growling?

Still, he had mentioned the word "lunch," the mother lode of all motivators. I reached out, grabbed the door handle, shook it as hard as I could, and then turned to my son. "Don't worry, Mommy will get us out of here somehow. I'm not spending my entire Mommy's Day locked in a closet," I said, offering reassurance as he calmly reached over, turned the door handle and opened the door. "Now why didn't *I* think of that?" I said. The two of us ran downstairs in pursuit of lunch.

"Where have you been?" my husband asked.

I started to answer when my child chimed in. "We've been having a Mommy's Day *potty* in the closet, Daddy."

*S*herry McCaulley Palmer is a published author who has enjoyed creative writing since childhood. Raised in Louisville, Kentucky, Sherry currently lives in the mountains of Eastern Tennessee with her husband, Brad, a Presbyterian minister, and her wonderful son, Charley, who provide much of the inspiration for her stories and poetry.

16

Plus Column

by Cheryl Pacilio

Not many of us moms are still available for volunteer work once the kids are in high school. Even those of us who made the sacrifice and enthusiastic commitment to stay at home during the elementary years find the siren song of career and college funding hard to resist once the kids are in their teens. And even if we don't heed that call, many of us have learned to eagerly anticipate the end of our PTO (Parent Teacher Organization) reigns. But today I went back to high school with my third child and had a really fun day.

I took a little time in the last years to reenter the workforce part time, change up my volunteer commitments from school to church to community, and even went back to graduate school. A move last year altered my career trajectory—and required me to relocate my dreams as well as my family—and it also gave me the privilege to experience full-time at-home mom status again. And I mean privilege. Something about taking care of my family feels really good this time around.

So this morning, as in all recent mornings, I woke up with my husband, listened for my early bird son's shower running, and jostled my high schooler six or eight times while her alarm blasted into sleep-deaf ears. But unlike other days, when I throw on old clothes to shuffle out on the trail with my pooch or sort piles of lights and darks, I had a reason to shower and make up my face. I even picked out an outfit that was cute enough (I hoped) to be approved by my teen. I was going to high school.

I headed downstairs to let out the dog, pour the orange juice, and start the sacred urn of coffee. Sometimes I'm too drowsy to scoop and grind and measure without leaving a mess on the counter, but today I'm a machine. It's a good day. I hand a cup off to my husband as he blows out the door. I start cooking the power breakfast that is a signature in our house when stamina will be required for the agenda. It's finals day at the high school—and this is brain food.

I whip together a lunch for the younger son, and set out the makings of his favorite cereal. He is a happy guy, and his singing from the nearby room makes this a doubly good morning. I jot a lunch box note—one that will undoubtedly make his eyes roll when he finds it, but also something that never fails to show up on Mother's Day cards. That reinforcement keeps me jotting—so far I've been making lunches for nearly 20 years! Yikes!

The high schooler comes down, nervous but ready early enough to eat sitting down for a change. "Mmm, this is good, Mom." Music to my ears. When she's finished I pour my coffee in a to-go cup and we head out for my leg of the car pool. As we pick up the first teenage neighbor—my high schooler notices the outfit I'm wearing. "You look cute, Mom. Did you go shopping?" Is the sun shining brighter just now, or is that just me? After two more pick ups, we head to the high school—just ahead of the busses that usually hold us hostage. Today we lead the yellow caravan and arrive on time—even early and I park the car. "Are you staying, Mom?" the high schooler asks.

"Yep. I'm passing out finals day treats and checking in textbooks this morning."

"Cool!"

It is cool. I get to meet other moms. I get to rub shoulders with some of the staff. I get to walk the halls my daughter walks every day. I get to see why it takes a full eight and not the allotted seven minutes to get from biology to the gym, feel the tension of halls pulsating with adolescent competition, pass girls in beautiful, expensive clothes and boys with intimidating bravado. I get to see the friends from the neighborhood, the dance studio, and church in a congealed environment. I get to hear them call me by name and wave to say hi. I get to see my daughter from across the lunchroom looking confident and cute and cramming for Spanish. It is very cool indeed!

Once in a while it's easy to count your blessings. I'm blessed to be a mom, blessed to be available, even blessed to volunteer at high school. Today was one of those plus-column days for me, and I actually enjoyed doing the math.

heryl is the quarter-century wife of Mike and mom of four children ranging in age from 23 to 12. They make their home in Geneva, Illinois. She is a teacher by vocation, a Bible studier by avocation, a Hearts at Home staffer, and an honest pal to her invaluable mom friends.

17

Getting Over an Overnight

by Julie Kaiser

Y ou never fully appreciate the importance of a child's attachments until they disappear.

We can relate. My husband and I each sleep with favorite pillows. Mine is a sentimental choice, a round pillow with pink accents my mom used to decorate the first bedroom I didn't have to share with anyone else. My husband's pillow isn't old, but it is properly squishy, claiming the same easily accessible spot every night.

Both of our children have connected with stuffed animals. Dog E. Dog arrived in our household shortly after our son did. His fur is now matted and his poor neck has been squeezed so tightly at night that there's hardly any stuffing left to hug. I once took Dog to a seamstress and asked if she could carefully reinsert some stuffing into his neck.

"He's a hardy dog," I said. She looked at me as though I were crazy and flatly refused.

A couple of years ago we accidentally left Dog behind at Grandma and Grandpa's house, an hour north of our home. We called immediately, trying to set up a drop-off at the midway point between our houses. While sympathetic to our plight, their schedule was full until two days later.

"Dog is having an overnight at Grandma and Grandpa's," we explained to our son, who eventually stopped crying and fell asleep.

The next morning a FedEx truck pulled up to our house and delivered Dog, all snugly packed into a little box, no worse for wear.

If our son's Depression-era grandparents hesitated a moment at the expense of overnighting a small, slightly bedraggled stuffed animal to our home, they never let on.

"We're just glad he got there so quick," they said when we called to thank them.

Our daughter's attachment to Sleepy Bear is no less intense. Sleepy recently disappeared on Easter morning, leaving our sugar-wired two-year-old bereft and inconsolable at naptime. I suspect she was using the situation to further her drama queen histrionics, but nevertheless, we turned the house upside down, room by room, pile by pile, to no avail.

"Where's Sleepy Bear?" she wailed, while I tried to cajole her into falling asleep.

My husband leaped into action, returning to church to comb through the nursery in search of the missing bear. No Sleepy, but there was a remarkably similar bear sitting on the shelf.

You'd think a person in a house of God would take a minute to ponder the potential consequences of pilfering a small stuffed bear, but I'm pretty sure the only thing he was contemplating was whether or not we could pass the thing off as Sleepy.

"That's not Sleepy," she said firmly after one glimpse of the imposter.

"You're right," I told her. "This is Sneezy...Sleepy's brother, all the way from church to give you a hug."

As parents, you want to make everything all right for your children. You want them to have the things that comfort for as long as they need them, no matter what anyone else thinks or how excruciating the location process when they become lost.

Sleepy eventually was discovered—zipped into a toy purse—and calm was restored to our household.

Dog has gone to kindergarten several times for show and share, but I know the day will come when Dog's boy will lose interest. The same fate awaits Sleepy too, someday. But I have made contingency plans for these beloveds.

They will sit on our bed, tucked between two favorite pillows, until their owners grow up to remember...and reclaim them.

*J*ulie Kaiser is glad to be a mom because the on-the-job training is like nothing she's ever experienced before... and her kids amaze her even when they are driving her insane. Julie and her husband, Scott, enjoy parenting their two children: Jakob (six) and Laura Grace (three).

18

The Mystery Man

by Brenda Poinsett

Row, row, row your boat,
 Gently down the stream.
Merrily, merrily, merrily, merrily,
 Life is but a dream.

The sounds of singing from the bathroom reached me as I sat in the living room of our small house. My husband, Bob, was bathing our two toddlers, and I loved listening to the sounds of boats splashing, boys laughing, and voices singing.

This time each day was Bob's gift to me. He took over the evening responsibilities of bathing the boys and putting them to bed while I relaxed in a comfy chair. Knowing my day's work of cleaning, cooking, and child care was finished made it a sweet time that I relished, but it was more than that.

As I sat with my feet up and a magazine in my lap, I often looked up from my reading and listened to their chatter and laughter. I thought this interaction time Bob was having with the boys was indicative of what a good job Bob and I were doing as parents. They were sure to rise up and thank us some day!

I thought this would be especially true of the investment Bob was making with their bathtime play. It would surely be one of the things Jim and Joel would recall when they were older because it was definitely quality time.

Eventually we moved away from that little house into a bigger one. By that time, the boys were old enough to take their own baths. Their interaction with Bob became more of a boisterous outside thing—playing catch, kicking a soccer ball, and shooting baskets when Bob got a chance. We had moved to a country home that required more work. His job was in the city, and the commute one-way was 45 minutes long. This job was more demanding and with longer hours than when Jim and Joel were small.

Life had changed for me as well because by this time we had a third child. When Ben was born, my workload increased considerably, especially after he started walking. Because of Bob's longer hours, my days with the children were longer, and I was not interacting much with other women because of our isolated location. I'll admit there were days when I watched the clock, anxious for Bob to get home for some adult conversation and some parenting relief.

Bob, remembering the special bath times he had with Jim and Joel when they were toddlers, wanted to recreate that scene with Ben. He tried very hard, but often his homecoming was so late I would already have Ben bathed and in bed.

One night, though, I was just too tired to give Ben a bath. It was one of those days mothers sometimes have when you begin to think you can't handle one more thing. Giving Ben a bath would have been that one more thing. I just didn't have the energy. Instead I settled in the family room with the three boys, and that's where I was when Bob arrived home. He too was tired and sat down on the couch beside me. We talked some but mostly sat quietly. Neither of us moved to give Ben a bath, and yet we could tell by his fretfulness that he was ready for bed. As I kept thinking I ought to get up and do something, an idea occurred to me. *Joel is eight and Jim is ten. Why can't one of them give Ben a bath?*

"Would one of you help us out and give Ben a bath tonight?"

"No way," said Joel.

"Not me," said Jim.

"Well, when you two were small there was a man who gave you a bath every evening. It was a special time. This man bathed you, played with you, sang with you, and scrubbed you squeaky clean. Since this man was so nice to you, why don't you do the same thing for your brother?"

Joel asked, "Who was that man?"

What? Bob and I looked at each other. We couldn't believe our ears. Joel didn't remember those special times that we thought were so significant, and even Jim didn't jump in with, "That was Dad. Don't you remember?"

That was the day I learned not to take parenting so seriously. You can do it all right and still not make a lasting impression! It was a good lesson to learn. It helped us enjoy our children more. It wasn't so much about how they were going to turn out and whether they would remember what we had done; it was about enjoying them. To this day, our three grown children don't remember those special bathtimes, but Bob and I do. I'll always remember how nice it was to have a husband who gave me an evening gift, and the sounds of the gift will always reverberate in my memory. My children may not rise up to call me blessed, but I'll always be blessed by having been their mother.

renda Poinsett is the wife of Bob and mother of Jim, Joel, and Ben. Now that her sons are grown, they may not remember memorable family times, but Brenda does and she writes about them in her books *Celebrations That Touch the Heart* and *Can Martha Have a Mary Christmas?*

19

Bless This Mess

by Becky Wiese

I couldn't stand it anymore…my feet stuck to the floor with every step I took. So there I was, mopping my kitchen floor at midnight. I felt somewhat comforted by the fact that mopping by moonlight meant the floor would stay clean longer than the usual 20-minute (if I'm lucky) span.

Unfortunately, the light of day seemed to highlight the rest of the mess…the toys on the floor, the dust on the piano, the fingerprints on the windows, the toothpaste stuck to the sink…and, of course, once breakfast was over, the mess on the kitchen floor (again).

The truth is, living with children is messy business.

Before I had my own kids, I had the naive (I would say "stupid," but that word is a no-no at our house) idea that at-home moms had very clean houses. After all, they were home all day, right? Now I know from experience that I was wrong on two counts: The first is we are not usually home all day, every day. It's hard to clean when you're not even there. The second is when we are home, so are our kids. It didn't take me very long to realize that a clean house and children are somewhat mutually exclusive.

I've recently come to terms with the simple facts of this particular season of life. I still clean my house, but now my expectations are different. Instead of expecting the toys to stay in their appointed position on a shelf for days on end, I'm satisfied when the pieces are somewhat together and not scattered in the middle of the floor. Instead of believing the bathroom mirror will stay spotless after working so hard to get all the toothpaste splatters and smears cleaned off, I'm content to know that my children are at least brushing their teeth.

And, although my kitchen floor doesn't stay clean for very long, I'm thankful that my kids are good (though somewhat messy) eaters.

It's taken me a while to realize that stressing out about the cleanliness of my windows, floors, and furniture is not worth the time and energy it takes to be upset about it. That's not what really matters, anyway. The truth is, our kids will appreciate the time we spend with them so much more than spotless floors and sparkling windows.

Really, what's more important: vacuuming the carpet or playing catch? Cleaning the bathroom or reading books? Dusting the furniture or speculating on life during the time of dinosaurs?

It can be hard to find the balance between being available to our kids and teaching them that cleaning the house and other chores and responsibilities are important too. Sometimes the answer is to put off the chore for a while to play. Other times a compromise works better: Set a time limit to finish the task and then join in the fun. There are even times when the answer is to ask for their help. And, of course, there is always the option of the midnight cleaning shift.

Yes, someday my house will be clean. I look forward to that time with anticipation and sadness. Anticipation because the floors will not be sticky, the windows will sparkle and the walls won't be smudged. Sadness because when that season of cleanliness arrives, my children will be gone…off on their own to make and clean their own messes.

I want my kids to know that they are more important than my kitchen floor. I want to take the time to read, play, and laugh with my children while they are young because if I do, they'll be more likely to want to come to me for help, encouragement, support, and, yes, even fun stuff when they are older.

And that's worth any mess!

> ecky and her husband, Mike, are the parents of four active children, ages 16 to 8. In her "spare" time, she enjoys reading, writing, watching her children's sporting events, and participating in several sports herself. For obvious reasons, cleaning the house is not among her favorite activities, given its never-stay-clean-for-long odds.

Decisions, Dilemmas, and Determination

20

Pillow Fright

By Deborah Raney

Our oldest daughter, Tobi, was our strong-willed child. We recognized her independent spirit and her stubborn will almost from the day she was born. While we were living through the challenges of raising a spirited little girl like Tobi, it wasn't always easy to see the humor in things. Fortunately, hindsight has allowed us to see many of those struggles of will in a different light.

One afternoon, when Tobi was at the height of her fiery preadolescent years, she became furious with me because I wouldn't grant her permission to do something. (Of course, neither of us can even remember what it was now!) But, as usual, Tobi started throwing a fit, slamming doors and slapping books loudly on the kitchen table.

I did my best to keep my cool, but I could feel my blood pressure rising and knew I was in danger of losing my own temper. Through clenched teeth, I tried to reason with her. "Tobi Anne, settle down right now. You are going to ruin something and then we will both be sorry." My words did little to calm her, and finally I took her by the shoulders and gently but firmly "escorted" her to her room.

As we marched down the hall, I had a sudden flashback of myself as a preteen. I had almost forgotten that I'd kicked a door or two myself back in those days when things didn't go my way.

An idea struck and I reached for the pillow on Tobi's bed. "You know, honey, I remember when I was your age that if I got angry, I sometimes used to feel like hitting something too, so I understand your need to get your frustrations out. But if you feel like you just have to punch something, it needs to be something you can't hurt."

"Here," I told her, handing her the pillow. "You can punch your pillow to your heart's content." She took it from me, and I left the room.

All was quiet for quite some time, and I was just about to congratulate myself on my brilliant handling of the situation, when I heard the muffled sound of fist meeting pillow again and again.

Nevertheless, Tobi emerged from her room a few minutes later, cool, calm, and collected. I smiled smugly to myself and forgot the incident until about a week later.

It was wash day and I was methodically stripping all the beds in the house. I came to Tobi's room and started taking the sheets off her bed. Stripping off the pillowcase, I found myself face-to-face with a larger-than-life portrait rendered directly onto the pillow in colorful marking pens.

Now, you need to understand that Tobi inherited some of her father's remarkable artistic talents, and this portrait was quite skillfully done. In fact, the face on the pillow looked vaguely familiar.

And then it struck me. It was my own face staring back at me!

As I pictured my daughter methodically drawing my likeness on her pillow and then beating the stuffings out of "me" with her fists, I laughed so hard I could barely finish the laundry. I couldn't help but be impressed with her creativity—and with the willpower it must have taken not to show me her handiwork the moment it was completed.

I have no doubt that her portrait punching bag was well used for the remainder of her years at home. (Just for the record, the only punishment we ever doled out for defacing the pillow came a few months later when brand-new pillows were purchased for the family during a discount store white sale. I bought only five pillows for our six-member family. Tobi didn't even have to ask why she wasn't the recipient of a new one.)

When Tobi went away to college a few years later, I'm pretty sure her punching bag pillow went with her. But I'd be willing to bet, from the sweetness and love we heard in her voice through 400 miles of telephone wire, that her punching bag pillow got hugged more than hammered.

We've told the pillow story many times over the years, and Tobi laughs loudest of all—especially now that she's a mommy herself. Our little grandson is mild mannered and sweet, but Tobi and her husband are expecting their second baby soon, and she confesses that she's a tiny bit fearful that the Lord just might think she deserves a strong-willed child of her own.

I say, as long as that baby grows up to be as precious as his mother, it will be worth every struggle.

Deborah Raney's novels have won the RITA Award, HOLT Medallion, National Readers' Choice Award, and Excellence in Media's Silver Angel. Her first novel inspired the World Wide Pictures' film *A Vow to Cherish*. Deb and her husband, Ken, have a teenager, three grown children, and are now enjoying two grandbabies.

21

A Touch Toward Transitioning

by Mary Byers

My first pregnancy coincided with a job I loved. I didn't want to give it up. Consequently, I was thrilled when a woman at our church agreed to accept my daughter into her in-home day care. I felt blessed.

Then I became pregnant with my second child and things seemed more complicated. Getting one child out the door in the morning was tough enough. How would I find time for a demanding job that required travel, grocery shopping, house cleaning, soccer games, Little League, dance lessons, etc.? Lots of women I knew were burning the candle at both ends and were perpetually exhausted.

I began to feel that God was calling me to stay home with my children. When a friend reported that she was leaving work to be home with her kids, I was shocked. After all, the generation of women before me won the right for us to work, not stay home and bake cookies! And what did stay-at-home moms do all day, anyway? (Looking back, I'm ashamed of myself for ever asking this question.)

I went to my friend and asked, "Why are you leaving your job? What about your career long term? Don't you think you'll be bored?"

I quizzed her even harder after she had been home for a while. "How are you managing? What's it like being home with little people all day?" Her answers were calm and certain. She loved being home with her kids.

I began to wonder if staying home was what God wanted for me too. But would I really have the courage to leave my job behind? While I prayed, I looked for alternatives. I took out a large piece of paper and began brainstorming possibilities—from finding a part-time job, asking for flextime, or freelancing from home to not working at all. The latter alternative frightened me because I had never pictured myself at home with children. But I continued to feel that God was calling me to have the courage to do something I never dreamed I'd do.

I pondered the possibilities. I prayed about it. I held fast to Jeremiah 29:11: "'For I know the plans I have for you,' declares the LORD, 'plans to prosper you and not to harm you, plans to give you hope and a future.'" I read, and reread, Ecclesiastes 3:1: "There is a time for everything, and a season for every activity under heaven." Could it be that God was calling me to a season of child rearing?

It took me almost a year to make my decision. As the year progressed, it became clear that God *was* calling me to a home office. My husband and I began to squirrel away money in preparation for the change, and I began the move in my mind from a senior-level staff member to "Vice President of Intergenerational Development," the title I gave myself to help with the transition.

I left my job with fond farewells and amid good wishes. I was able to do some freelance work during naptimes and, thanks to my husband's generous vacation schedule, was also able to accept paid speaking engagements, which I had been doing before I left full-time employment. When I had an engagement, my husband would take the day off and be home with the kids while I worked. It seemed like the perfect solution. And yet I still had doubts.

Like other working mothers, I burned the candle at both ends. I accepted too many writing assignments and found myself up late at night—and then grumpy and ineffective with the children the next morning. I had to turn down interesting work in order to achieve balance, but saying no didn't come easily to me and made me feel I was missing out and not living up to my potential. True, my plan to be available to my children was working, but not as smoothly as I'd hoped. And so I turned to God again in prayer.

"Lord," I cried desperately one morning as the kids and I rushed out the door to take my daughter to preschool. "How come I'm doing such a miserable job finding a balance between being a mom and working from home? If this is where You want me, how come it doesn't feel like it?" I listened for an answer but didn't hear anything. I felt very alone.

After dropping my daughter off at preschool, my son and I returned home. Instead of the usual rush to get work done, I decided to take a walk with him. He reached up and took my hand, and I looked down at the child who was so dependent on me—and loved me no matter what my priorities were. As I watched our shadows walk hand in hand before us on the sidewalk, I found the answer I had been seeking. I realized things weren't running smoothly because my priorities were in the wrong order. I focused on business first, my family second. Watching my son's small shadow walk with mine made me realize that family had to come first.

As Keri Wyatt Kent writes in *God's Whisper in a Mother's Chaos,* "We expect a divine smack in the head, so we're oblivious to the divinity of the touch of our child's hand in ours as we cross the street." My own smack in the head actually came *via* the touch of my son's hand in mine.

It's been six years since I've reordered my priorities. During that time, I've had many wonderful moments with my children. I've also written three books and watched my speaking business grow. And I learned an important lesson: When your priorities are in proper order, it's easier for everything else to fall in place.

ary M. Byers is the author of *How to Say No…and Live to Tell About It*. She's a frequent media guest on women's topics and speaks professionally to a wide variety of audiences. Mary and her husband, Stuart, live in central Illinois with their two youngest children.

22

The Fearful What-Ifs

by Megan Kaeb

Kory, I'm not going," I told my husband as tears filled my eyes one evening the week before we were scheduled to leave the country on a short-term mission trip to Ukraine. A swarm of thoughts buzzed through my brain. We were going to spend ten days away from our children on the other side of the world. Fear gripped me. At that moment, the risks of going seemed too great.

What-ifs started to attack me: What if something happens to them? What if something happens to us? Unfortunately the what-ifs didn't stop there; instead, they grew in size and specificity. What if our kids are miserable without us? What if they make their babysitters miserable? What if they run in front of cars? What if they go to a park and get kidnapped? What if terrorists take over our plane? What if our kids have to grow up without parents?

I was making myself miserable, but I couldn't seem to stop. This wasn't the first time we were leaving our kids. And it wasn't the first time I was leaving the country. When our daughter was a one-year-old, we went on a mission trip to Ukraine. I remember it was hard to leave her then, but we went. Not only that—we returned home alive.

I remember one day in particular that first trip. It was a Sunday and a couple sat in front of us holding a one-year-old girl. I had to hold back tears throughout the service as I listened to a message in a language I couldn't understand while watching a little girl who reminded me so much of my own. I felt homesick. All I wanted at that moment was to go home. But God spoke to my heart and asked me to trust Him with my little girl. I knew He had called me on this trip. I needed to trust that He was in control. It was a good lesson for me to learn and a moment I have not forgotten.

It was a lesson I needed to be reminded of again. I remember feeling those same irrational fears and what-ifs before our first trip to Ukraine, and here I was, years later, feeling them again. In my heart I knew I couldn't make a decision based on fear. An old memory verse kept running through my head: "Perfect love casts out fear (1 John 4:18 NKJV). I knew my what-ifs were not coming from God.

I like to think I am in control of my children when I am home with them. The reality is, I have no control. Those what-ifs could happen whether I am at home or out of the country. I knew I needed to put my children in God's hands and trust that He was in control. Although that didn't stop me from praying I would break my arm or that something not too tragic would happen just before we left so I wouldn't have to go on the trip.

Thankfully, my husband didn't take me seriously when I informed him I wasn't going. He let me voice my fears and let God remind me who was really in control. Although I could not muster much excitement for the trip, I felt the peace that passes all understanding come over me as I surrendered my children to God's care.

The following week went by in a flash with no arm-breaking accidents to give me an excuse to stay home. Before I knew it, I was on an airplane headed to Ukraine with my kids at home in the care of trusted sitters. The week ended up being a success on both sides of the world. Although our kids were excited to see us when we returned, apparently they didn't miss us too much while we were gone. In fact, they had a great ten days without us.

And we had a great ten days without them. We developed special relationships with the people we met and felt God's hand on the trip. God was even able to use my fears in a positive way. I was asked to give a short testimony at a church we visited. I told them how I was fearful to leave my children at home, how I did not want to come to Ukraine. And I told them how God spoke to me. I told them that if I wanted my children to be willing to serve God and make sacrifices for Him, I needed to be willing to do that myself. I encouraged them to do the same.

The trip to Ukraine reminded me again that my children are not my own. They are precious gifts entrusted to me for a short time from God. I am not in control, but God is, and He can be trusted. Someday we hope to make another trip to Ukraine. If we leave our children behind, I am sure I will be bombarded again by the fearful what-ifs. But I also know that God is in control, and He will help me through it.

egan serves as the director of publishing for Hearts at Home, but her most important job is wife to Kory and mom to their four children. In her spare time she loves to read and encourage other moms through her blog (whadusay2.blogspot.com). She is so glad to be a mom.

23

How It's "Supposed" to Be

by Jody Antrim

Is this a Mr. or Mrs. Antrim?"

My initial thought out of my sound sleep was why would a salesperson call at this hour? But that notion quickly changed when I discovered the caller was a nurse at a hospital two hours away—more specifically, a hospital with my 20-year-old daughter in their emergency room. There'd been a car accident. This was not going to be an ordinary day.

I absorbed as much as I could while simultaneously praying, and then I shared the details with my husband. The nurse instructed us to remain at home until the doctors could determine a plan. I had to do that difficult task mothers are so often called on to do…wait.

That day marked the beginning of a month-long journey back to some sense of normalcy. Two hospitals (with a helicopter ride to transport my "little girl" between them), four days in ICU, two weeks in a city hospital two hours from home, broken bones and collapsed lungs, all happened when our Kristin was "supposed to be" taking semester exams, hanging out with her college friends, and looking forward to a nice Christmas break. I, on the other hand, was "supposed to be" decorating our home for Christmas, preparing for the arrival of our two daughters home from college, shopping, and getting ready for the four of us to fly to Pennsylvania for Christmas with my parents.

"Supposed to be" is one of those phrases you have to learn to rethink when you're a mom.

We all like stories with a happy ending. Yes, we did get to bring our Kristin home just two days before Christmas. But even though there had been many life lessons along the way, it was on December twenty-third—the day we arrived home after two weeks away—that we were given the biggest and most unexpected lesson of all.

During our long drive back home, I spoke to my husband and grown daughters about how this Christmas would be oh-so-not-ordinary. I could think of only one thing on my "supposed to do" list that had actually been accomplished—and that only halfheartedly. A friend had insisted on taking me Christmas shopping for a little break away from my daughter's hospital bed, and she kindly offered to bring the few packages back to her home for safekeeping. But that was all I had done to prepare for this special holiday. Although this was "supposed to be" the case, there would be no tree, no decorations, no possibility of attending our traditional Christmas Eve service at church, and no way to be surrounded by our extended family as planned. I wanted everyone braced for a very plain Christmas—the four of us would quietly celebrate that we were all together. It would be good...just not the Christmas we would ordinarily expect. Little did I know what was in store for our family on that day.

As we turned into our driveway, you couldn't miss it. Shining through our front picture window was a tree radiant with white lights. We entered through our kitchen door and discovered a fully decorated room and, on the counter, a handwritten note. It welcomed us home and informed us that there would be meals delivered each day for the next two weeks—the arrival of our first homemade dinner was just an hour away. We stepped from the kitchen into the living room, and there was a sprinkling of wrapped gifts under a tree covered with ornaments and lights! How could all of this have happened without our knowing? And an even bigger question for me—how could all of this have happened without *my* doing a thing...me, the director of operations in our home?

We quickly learned that our circle of friends—all part of our church—had ingeniously found their way into our home, dug through our not-so-cleaned up basement to find the Christmas decorations (eek!), and transformed our home with what was undeniably an extraordinary dose of love. That friend who had taken me shopping? She knew who the gifts were for and she wrapped them up and made them a sight to behold!

Not one of us will ever forget it. To this day our daughter Emily says that "Joes to Go"—the homemade sloppy joes that arrived our first night home—is one of her favorite dishes. Many of Kristin's memories include physical pain—but some of them are good. One of her Christmas gifts from her sister was the children's game Operation, and it hurt those broken ribs of hers to laugh as they played.

The events of December 1999 were yet another reminder that being a mom doesn't always go as it's "supposed to." I can't point to the moment when I felt assured that things would be all right—that our daughter would heal and we'd look back at that time as simply a speed bump.

What I do know is that for a mother to be there for her family, she doesn't do it alone. I looked to my husband to take care of the avalanche of legal, medical, and insurance papers. I looked to my oldest daughter to provide love, support, and extra hands. And our friends—that community that so generously gave of themselves—I learned I could look to them for extraordinary love that lifted us then and still carries us today. I believe that on December twenty-third, God orchestrated it all and taught me that's how it's "supposed to be."

*J*ody lives in Central Illinois and is wife to Bob (celebrating 35 years together!), mom to Emily and Kristin, mother-in-law to Carlos, and grandma to Emma and Isabel. In addition to her family, her list of loves includes: speaking, writing, serving as a marriage mentor, Hearts at Home activities, hosting parties, and time with friends.

24

Stuck

by Marcia Jordon

It was the day I had been dreading; the day I realized I couldn't fix the problem alone. I was forced to humble myself and call in the big guns, all because of a simple child's building block table.

The day started out very normal. My husband left for work, carpooling with a friend who worked in the same city. I was at home with our two sons, Joseph who was three and Jacob who was four months. The morning followed our typical pattern. Dress Joseph. Nurse Jacob. Feed Joseph breakfast. Nurse Jacob. Play with Joseph. Nurse Jacob.

It was during one of these "nurse Jacob" moments when I heard the words that would change our day. "I'm tuck, Mama," Joseph called from the other room.

I set Jacob down in his bouncy seat and walked around the corner to the next room. There, standing in a hole in the middle of the block table was Joseph. He appeared to be wearing the table as a skirt. The hole, intended for a small bucket to hold building blocks, instead held Joseph. He was stuck and could not get out!

I began trying to pull him out by holding the table down with one knee. I knew right away that this would not work. So I tried the next logical thing—to push him back through the hole. I had Joseph put one arm down through the hole to try to make room for his other arm to go through, but this too proved unsuccessful. And instead of loosening him, it lodged him even tighter! Now instead of standing in the middle of the table, he was crouching under it with his head, two shoulders and one arm above it. He was most emphatically s-t-u-c-k.

Panic started to set in. I dialed my husband's work number and explained the situation to him. When he finished laughing he suggested I try something slippery to help slide him out. So I went to the kitchen, found the canola oil, and slathered Joseph's upper chest and shoulder. It didn't help. Next he suggested I cut him out with a hacksaw. Another good idea if we knew where the saw could be found.

I was beginning to feel desperate. Because Jason had carpooled to work, he was unable to come to our rescue. I was on my own, and Joseph was starting to get uncomfortable and scared. I found a favorite piece of blanket to comfort and keep him calm. It was quiet on the other end of the phone as my husband thought. Then he spoke the words I had been dreading. "You're going to have to call the fire department."

"No!" I protested. But despite my protest, I knew he was right. I could not fix the situation on my own, and my little boy was stuck. It was time to swallow my pride and call for help.

I calmly explained to Joseph that I could not get him out and that I was going to ask some firemen to come and rescue him. As I continued to reassure him that everything would be all right, I found the non-emergency phone number for our local fire department and dialed.

The woman on the other end was very nice as I explained our situation. I could hear the smile in her voice as she repeated back what I had described. "You have a three-year-old child who is stuck in the middle of a building block table?"

"Yes, ma'am," I said. A moment later she informed me that a truck was on its way.

Then in true mother-like fashion, I took stock of the situation.

Ugh. My living room and dining room could use a good cleaning, I thought, followed by *Why, oh, why is Joseph only in a Pull-Up?*

I carefully moved Joseph—and the table—into the main part of the living room where he would be more accessible to the firemen. Within a few minutes, a fire engine pulled up in front of our home and two burly men came to my front door. They had big grins on their faces as they looked at poor Joseph and reassured him that they would get him out.

They decided after some discussion that the hacksaw would be the best option and informed me that my table would have to be cut.

"Whatever it takes! The table is the least of my concerns," I replied as I snapped a quick picture of Joseph before they began sawing. This was a moment that needed to be documented!

They had Joseph out of the table within 15 minutes. Once I got him properly dressed, the firemen took him out to sit in the big red fire engine. Joseph was thrilled. As they got ready to leave, we thanked them for coming to our rescue. They assured me that this was the kind of call they enjoyed responding to. Joseph had made their day.

That fateful morning has served as a reminder that it is okay if I don't have all the answers. Joseph and I both survived, and I learned that it is okay to ask for help. It is a day that will forever stand out in my mothering journey, the day that Joseph got stuck!

*M*arcia Jordon has been married to her husband, Jason, for 13 years, and they have three sons, Joseph (eight), Jacob (five), and Jesse (three). She loves being a homeschooling mom and pastor's wife, and in her "free time" she enjoys scrapbooking and reading.

25

I Can't Do It! I Can't Do It! I Did It!

by Melissa Herter

From day one I have taken my job as a mother seriously. Some of my friends and family call me a perfectionist. I want to succeed at everything I do, and if I'm not successful, I can at least rest knowing I gave it everything I had.

Now that I'm a mother, I try to instill those traits of persistence, drive, and ambition into my children. I don't expect them to breeze through high school in one year or become geniuses at age 13. And I'm not one of those mothers who puts my children into positions for automatic failure, like enrolling them in a swimming relay while they're still in water wings. But I do expect them to use the talents that God has given them, try to do their best, and most importantly, try without complaining.

That said, there are two magic words that make both my husband and me cringe when we hear them: "I can't." Each time I hear "I can't" from my six- and eight-year-old sons, my stomach tightens and my blood pressure rises. I can just picture my sons' futures—never learning to drive, never learning to cook, never learning to do laundry, and perhaps worst of all, never leaving home!

Perhaps it is because I'm such a driven person that "I can't" causes such a stir in me. I think of how many times I've heard "I can't" from my children. "I can't find this" or "I can't reach that." How about: "I can't tie my shoes...I can't do it...I can't, I can't, I can't!" Can we please remove that phrase from our vocabulary, all together now?

But then the day came when I saw one of my children finally understand why "I can't" didn't have to remain his life's theme. When my oldest son was five, he announced he was ready to ride his bike like a big boy, without training wheels. A rush of emotions went through me. Excitement—my little boy was growing up. Fear—oh, how many times will he fall over before he finally gets the hang of it? Sympathy—for all of the skinned-up knees I would have to bandage. I took a quick check of the first aid supplies to be sure I could handle the need for bandages and ointment. And off we went to remove the training wheels and begin.

We knew the sidewalks in front of our house worked great for keeping the kids safe while riding bikes and playing. What we didn't realize was that the grass on the edges of the sidewalk could make trying to learn to ride a bike without training wheels resemble bumper bowling. So there we went, up and down the sidewalk. My son had his helmet secured, and I was running along beside him holding the handle bars and seat. I wasn't going to let him fall if it took every bit of motherly strength I had. How long could I keep him from falling on his own?

"I can't do it. I can't do it," my son said each time he would tip over beyond my reach and fall. Now, as I'm running with him and trying to keep him upright, I'm ignoring the digging into my legs of the pedal each time it goes around. I'm ignoring the tires as they roll over my feet again and again. Did I mention that the bandages and ointment were more for me than for my son?

After a few days of practicing up and down the sidewalk and many more "I can't do its," we accepted a friend's advice and drove our son and his bike to our church parking lot. It was empty, wide open, and free of obstacles—especially those sidewalk bumpers that had caused us so much trouble. When I told him it was time to saddle up and try again, he looked me in the eyes with tears and said once more, "I can't do it."

Here was my teaching moment! I explained to my son that none of us are born knowing how to do all of these things. It's through our strength and determination, and the love and grace of God, that we grow, learn, and, most of all, TRY! Off I went, running alongside again, holding him up so he wouldn't fall on the hot, hard asphalt (at least those grass sidewalk bumpers had provided a soft place to land). As I let go of the handle bars and then the seat, off my little boy went on his own, riding his bike without training wheels. He exclaimed with great joy, "I did it!" And so he had.

We followed the same plan when our second son learned to ride his bike. Except this time we avoided the sidewalk bumpers and headed straight for the parking lot.

My children have finally learned that if I hear the words "I can't do it," I always follow them with "Try it, and you CAN do it."

Amazingly enough, with God's help, they usually can.

Melissa Herter lives in Youngsville, Louisiana, with her husband of 13 years, Jason, and two sons, Grant (eight) and Drew (seven). She is a full-time working mother who enjoys spending time with her family, sports, being outdoors, and being number one cheerleader to her sons' many sports activities.

Faith of a Child

26

Sunglasses to See

by Danna Demetre

Rousing a four-year-old out of a deep sleep can be a challenge. It's a challenge for me to get up and at 'em on Sunday morning. And this Sunday we were running way behind schedule. I called out to my little boy as I entered his room. "Jesse, it's time to get up. It's Sunday. We're going to church. Jesus is waiting!"

Jesus is waiting. It just slipped out innocently. I had no idea the impact it would have on our entire day.

The first words out of his froggy little throat were, "He IS? Jesus is at church today?"

"Of course, sweetheart. Jesus is always at church," I responded.

"He IS?" he replied in wonder.

"Well, yes, Jesse. Jesus is everywhere. And He especially likes to be at church. So, let's get going or we'll be late!"

Ten minutes later he appeared in my bathroom as I made the last few cosmetic adjustments necessary to leave the house looking bright eyed and well rested. *Isn't makeup a wonderful thing?*

"Jesse, why are you wearing sunglasses?" I asked.

"So I can see Jesus better when we get to church."

"Honey, you can't see Jesus with your eyes…He's in your heart." *I hoped he understood.*

"But I want to SEE Jesus!"

Oh, the challenges of explaining the spiritual dimension to little ones. All morning at church, Jesse was peeking around corners and sleuthing into rooms like an espionage agent trying to sneak up on Jesus. I think that he had the impression that Jesus was playing some spiritual version of hide-and-seek. He just couldn't understand why Jesus would not reveal Himself physically.

Our usual routine after church is a quick trip to Starbucks. Jesse loves the activity and his own version of a decaf mocha. As my husband and I loaded him into the backseat, he continued his quest. "Will Jesus be at Starbucks too, Papa?"

"Well, I guess He will be if we're there. Because He never leaves us!" We hoped this fact didn't get out to the coffee bean giant. We could just see some celestial advertisement popping up with Jesus as the ultimate celebrity endorsement!

After coffee we took a quick jaunt into the local drugstore before heading home. "Is Jesus here too?" Jesse asked. We continued to try our best to explain that Jesus is always with us because we have asked Him into our lives. Jesse said, "I know Jesus is in my heart. But can I pull Him out from under my bones?"

In a cynical world it is so refreshing to watch the innocent discovery of a child seeking spiritual truth. As adults we become desensitized to the miracles of God. The technology of television, movies, and computers has dulled our senses to the real miracles of life. We've seen it all. And now the true spiritual dimension and miracles of the Bible are put in the same mental file cabinets often subconsciously labeled "fiction." Our minds have difficulty conceiving the intangible *unless* we get some spiritual help.

The Bible says that we will find God when we seek Him with all of our hearts (Jeremiah 29:13). He is real. He *is* tangible. No, not with our physical senses. But His Spirit will connect with ours when we seek Him with faith like a child. Jesus said in Luke 18:17 that anyone who will not receive the kingdom of God like a little child will never enter it.

And so I marveled at the faith of my curious, knee-scraped little guy, who never gave up all day Sunday looking for Jesus. We pulled into the garage, gathered up our packages, and helped Jesse out of the car when we finally got home that afternoon. He was the first of us to reach the back door into the house. Pulling it open, he yelled at the top of his little lungs, "JESUS, WE'RE HOME!"

Jesus was there waiting for us...as He *always* is. So, Jesse and I just plopped down on the steps leading upstairs and had a little talk with Him. We told Him how much we loved Him for dying for our sins. We thanked Him for loving us that much. We told Him we could feel His presence even if we couldn't see Him. I took a little peek at Jesse during our prayer time. He had one eye open watching for Jesus.

Jesus is here for you also. Can *you* see Him with your heart? If He seems far away or intangible, call out to Him just like Jesse. And He will respond...when you have the faith of a child.

*I*nternational speaker and author Danna Demetre loves teaching and encouraging women of all ages to embrace their identity in Christ. She and her husband, Lew, call San Diego home. In addition to two adult daughters, they are raising their adopted grandson, Jesse (now 11). You can reach Danna at: www.dannademetre.com.

27

Finding God in the Bathroom

By Lisa Boggs

Some of the best conversations I have with my children are in the bathroom. I still have not figured that one out. This conversation was no exception. Justine is eight years old and will ask you questions that you would think came from an adult. So when she began to comment on the Bible verses I have displayed on the mirror in my bathroom, I was not surprised.

"I like the one about the full armor of God," she said, referring to the words of Ephesians 6:10-17 that are posted on my mirror. I knew she liked that one—she still likes to watch her older brother's Bibleman tapes.

"But I don't like this one," she added, referring to Jeremiah 6:16, which happens to be my favorite. Justine then began to quote the verse in question to me with full expression: "This is what the LORD says: 'Stand at the crossroads and look. Ask for the *ancient* paths, ask where the good way is, and walk in it, and you will find rest in your souls.' *But you said, 'We will not walk in it'*" (emphasis added). I could tell by her expression that commentary was coming.

"Why would you want to walk on old roads? You should really

take out that last line. I don't like it." Once again I forgot I was talking to an eight-year-old and found myself answering as though I were talking to an adult.

"Oh, honey," I began, "that is the most important part of the verse. I could never take that out."

She responded with every child's favorite question: "Why?"

"Because I am the one who makes the choice. God can only show me what He wants me to do or where to go, but I am the one that has to follow the path He has given me." I was into it now and was not about to stop. "It is just like what Mommy does every day when I make choices about my food. I am the one who chooses to eat when I am not hungry and I am the one who chooses to eat past what I need. God does not make me do that."

It was then I noticed my daughter's jaw had dropped and her eyes were big. I knew I had forgotten she was only eight again, but I could not turn back now. "You make mistakes, Mommy?"

All I could do was smile. The innocence in her eyes was priceless. I sometimes forget that she still adores her parents and cannot believe we do anything wrong.

"Yes, I do," I finally said. "No one is perfect. Only Jesus was. I make mistakes every day. That is why it is important for me to remember every day that I must make the choice to do right or wrong. And I can't do that alone. I need to talk to God every day to keep me on the right path."

Justine still had the look of amazement in her eyes when she asked the next question. "Do you ever forget to pray like I do sometimes?"

I so badly wanted to tell her that I pray every day, but I knew in my heart that was not true. "No, I do forget sometimes. Sometimes instead of praying while I am doing something, I get so caught up in other things that I forget to talk to God. I don't like that about me. It is so important for me to pray before I do anything else, so I ask God to keep putting that desire in my heart. I pray that He puts it in your heart too."

"Mommy, I feel better when I pray."

"Me too."

Then I found myself praying with Justine. Asking God to help us do better at praying and spending time with Him. I do not remember praying like that with my mother when I was growing up. Knowing how and when to pray with my children had been a struggle for me. But that day in our bathroom, it came so easily, as though we had been praying like this since the moment Justine was born. I realized that it is not how or when we pray that matters. It is that we are praying together.

Some of my best conversations with my children are in the bathroom. It is where we found God.

*L*isa was thrilled when God chose Jason as her husband. Although her doctors believed she would never have children, she was able to be a stepmom to Ryan and Kendra. While applying for her master's of divinity she discovered God had a different plan—full-time motherhood. Justine joined their family in November of 1998, and since then Lisa has loved ministering to her own children and those in her church family.

28

Dinner Hour

By Elisa Pulliam

It was the dinner hour in my home. The famous hour across America known for cranky children, hungry bellies, and tired mommies. Although I've been at this mothering thing for more than seven years, I never fully appreciated the challenges most *normal* mothers face on a daily basis as they managed the dinner hour in their homes. In my *abnormal* experience, I spend the dinner hour with my family and more than 150 teenagers in a formal dining room where the food is brought right to our table. Carrying on conversation with teens while entertaining my children with crayons and fresh-baked bread doesn't exactly prepare one for fixing dinner at home alone with four youngsters.

As a part of my husband's employment teaching at a college prep boarding school, he is required to attend a portion of the meals served in the dining hall. Our family joins him and a handful of students at our assigned table by 6:15 p.m. sharp. The bell rings, grace is prayed, and tables are dismissed to get the first course. Our children's plates are served up first, giving me time to cut and dice while the platters are passed. Soon we're greeted by the maître d', dismissing us to take back plates and securing a person for cleanup at the end of the meal.

This is the wonderful signal announcing, "Last lap! The finish is in sight!" Finally, the doors open, declaring the meal is officially over. In case you missed it, the mad dash of teenagers running for carpet sweepers and spray bottles will knock you out of your seat, sending you and your little ones reeling out the door.

Bell. Grace. Serve. Dice. Eat. Dash. That is the pace of the dinner hour I've been trained to run, which did not prepare me for an unusual night home alone with my children. Hubby dear kissed me goodbye, off for a meeting, and I headed to the kitchen to fix dinner. The girls, then four and six, were playing upstairs. The twins, barely six months old, were quiet in their swings. I pulled out the pans, grabbed the can opener, dug around for the bread, and whisked out the butter and cheese. *Ah, beautiful,* I thought. *It is all coming together.* Until...

The twins began to fuss. I cranked up the swings. The girls were restless and suddenly under my feet. The burner was set too high. The soup was starting to bubble over. The twins' whimpers turned to cries. The girls kept chattering. Suddenly, I was in the throes of fixing dinner, answering questions, and clicking buttons on swings while trying to tame two hot burners from destroying my hearty meal of grilled cheese sandwiches and tomato soup.

The temperature was rising on more than just the stove. "Girls, just get to the table!" I insisted, pushing their commentary on my mounting culinary disaster into the dining room. For a split second all four of their adorable mouths were beautifully closed. Serenity lasted only for a moment, when my four-year-old proclaimed, "Mommy, isn't it too bad that mommies can't have daddies around all the time!" She was perceptive beyond her years. Her big sis came to the rescue and declared, "Why don't you call Grandma over to help? I bet she can come after work."

"I CANNOT ask for help! I always ask for help!" I adamantly confessed. "I have to do this on my own! God gave me all of you. I should be able to do it. Mothers fix dinner and manage kids all the time. Certainly I can."

Hmm. Can we say pride?

This was the first time since the twins were born that I even attempted to survive the dinner hour alone without the support of my mother, mother-in-law, sister, or husband.

"But, Mommy, God can do it for you!" My eldest knew I needed more than just my family; I needed the source of my strength. The four-year-old agreed. "Yes, God can help you!"

Grace.

"Dear Lord, I pray that You would bless this food. And I also pray for Mommy, that You would help her tonight. That the babies wouldn't cry. That You would bring her help," asked my tenderhearted daughter. Her lil' sis echoed, "Dear Father, I pray for Mommy. Please help her. Please, please make the babies not cry and make them sleep."

The meal continued quietly, followed by an unusually smooth bedtime routine. By 8:00 the twins were soundly asleep, not a tear shed for hours. I tucked the girls into bed, reminding them as I closed the door that "Jesus loves you and so do I." Suddenly, I was overwhelmed by the silence and washed in a wave of peace. I threw open the girls' door and declared, "Do you realize God answered your prayers tonight?"

Beautiful brown eyes, the color of rich chocolate, peered at me from above their quilts. "He did?" they chimed in together. "Yes! The babies didn't cry all evening. God gave me the strength to get through dinner and bedtime. He answered your prayers! He poured out His faithfulness on us. We have to remember this night that the Lord answered your prayers. Jesus really does love you and me too. Good night, girls."

"Good night, Mommy! We love you too." In their sweet words I heard the voices of angels singing out God's love to me—a tired, humbled-by-grace mother of four who just survived the dinner hour at home, but not alone. I was, indeed, a mommy overwhelmed by the grace of God, the strength of her Lord, wrapped in the arms of little ones who were not at all little in their faith.

*E*lisa is passionate about her vocation as wife and mother of four treasures. She also considers it a privilege to share about God's transforming love, especially with women and teenage girls, through relationships, writing/speaking, and her website, www.extravagantgrace.net. Elisa enjoys anything crafty or creative, laughing with her family, and friendships.

29

Scary Trust

by Tracie Elliot

I t used to be scary to trust God with my kids' prayers. I wanted my kids to learn that God answers prayer and that they should use prayer as a first resort, but I would worry that God wouldn't answer a prayer in the way they expected, and they would then lose faith. To me, it seemed a valid concern. Some of the prayers my kids shot up were unimportant, trivial, or just plain wild. I used to think God was too big for these little concerns. Boy, did He have a lesson for me!

Since I walk my two children, Mark (nine) and Sarah (six), to school about four blocks every day, we've gotten in the habit of saying prayers on our morning trip. We started this one morning because we were in a hurry and the practice stuck. I like our daily tradition because the kids learn they can pray anywhere and everywhere, even with their eyes open! We like to pray for the upcoming day, ask a blessing on their teachers, thank God for all He has given us, and express any concerns we have.

Well, the prayers I was hearing began to sound the same after a while, so I started talking to my kids about being specific when they pray. "Just talk to God about your lives," I'd tell them. "Pray about things that matter to you." I started modeling for them the everyday concerns we can bring to God. I prayed about a job possibility, a church member in the hospital, and worries I had about my busy schedule. They caught on and started to pray about a mean kid at school, a sick friend, or concern over a spelling test. This routine has become one of my favorite times of the day, and their prayers almost always make me smile. Almost...

On our walk to school, we pass by an abandoned house. The house has broken windows, a boarded-up front door, and weeds growing out of the gutters. No one cuts the lawn or trims the bushes. No one shovels the sidewalk or rakes the leaves. I sometimes complain about the house's state of disrepair. The fact that we can't even use the side-walk because it's so overgrown with bushes and covered with dead leaves really irritates me. I guess Mark grew tired of my complaining and decided to do something about it. He decided to pray about this house. In fact, he specifically asked God to send someone to clean up the yard and sidewalk so we could use it. This was one of those prayers that made me nervous. A prayer for an abandoned house! I knew that no one was going to clean up the yard to that eyesore. We've lived by that abandoned wreck for six years, and no one has touched the yard, ever. Two days in a row he prayed about it as I started formulating my explanation for God's silence on the matter.

I never needed to share my explanation; God had things under control. On the walk home from school that second day, there was a lawn service in the yard of the abandoned house trimming the bushes, mowing the lawn, raking the leaves, and cleaning the yard. I was in complete shock. I've spent six years complaining about the mess in that yard; my son spent two days praying about it and God answered his prayer.

The greatest lesson for me was Mark's attitude. He wasn't surprised at all. He responded to my shock with, "Mom, why are you surprised? I knew God would take care of it." I guess that's what we Christians call faith. The Bible tells us that if we have faith as small as a grain of mustard seed, we can move mountains (Matthew 17:20). Mark's faith moved an amazing mountain in my life that day.

That answered prayer was probably more for me than Mark. God taught me to trust Him with my children and their wild prayers. God cares about my kids, and He knows how to build faith in them better than I do. I don't need to formulate explanations for God's actions. He is big enough to handle whatever they throw His way. So I will keep teaching my children to pray as a first resort. Or, should I say, they will keep teaching me.

I've got a bigger problem now. I've learned that God honors the prayers of children, and Mark has recently started praying for a baby brother!

Tracie Elliott is the mother of Mark (nine) and Sarah (six) and wife of 14 years to David Elliott. She is a member of the Berean Bible Students, where she serves as worship director and runs the Pioneer Club program. Before becoming a mom, she taught high school English. She resides in Lombard, Illinois.

30

Ice-Cream Spills and Sons of God

by Wendy Arneson

Today I started out doing everything right. It was a great morning, and rather than hanging around in our pajamas, watching cartoons on the couch while eating Pop-Tarts, I motivated myself to be organized and make our day count. Everything was going smoothly. I got my three sons dressed and breakfasted, loaded them into the minivan, and headed to our local YMCA, where I wanted to get a workout in. The boys did great in the nursery, and I left the Y feeling like a strong, disciplined, together mom.

So I announced to my guys that we were on our way to get some ice cream. I had a coupon for a free latte, and thought I would give my terrific kiddos a special treat. Most moms I know don't let their kids eat ice cream in the car, but a few drops of ice cream here and there didn't bother me.

I pulled smiling up to the drive-through. When our order came to the window, I asked David to come up to the front of the van so he could hand out the ice cream. David, always quick to help, jumped up to get the snacks. He gave Johnny his cone and then reached to give baby Sammy his ice-cream treat—only he did not watch to see if Sammy grabbed on to it. Ice cream fell to the floor, leaving a sticky mess between the door and the seat. At the same time, I was handing David his chocolate sundae, which he dropped because he was distractedly watching Sam's ice cream puddle up.

"Whoops! I'm sorry, Mommy," the little culprit said.

But, alas, the strong, disciplined, together mom had just left the car.

I brought the car to a stop, grabbed a handful of wet wipes, and started to give my son an earful while I cleaned. "Do you see how you weren't paying attention, David? This is what happens! This is the reason why you need to pay attention and look at people. I don't just tell you to look at people in the face to be polite, I tell you because it is necessary for you to know what they are saying and what is going on. You need to look when people hand you things and when you hand things to other people—you don't just let go. And now look at this mess! I was trying to be nice and give you a treat…" and on and on and on.

Poor David sat in his seat with the remains of his sundae in his cup holder. His big brown eyes were scared and sad as he took in my tirade. I huffed and puffed as I got back into the driver's seat with the sticky wipes. Then I looked back at David and told him to go ahead and eat his sundae as I thought to myself how lucky he was there was any left after the mess he made!

Johnny, sitting next to David and enjoying his ice cream cone (and the fact that he had nothing to do with this particular episode), called out, "Mommy, say, 'I forgive you, David.' And David, you say, 'Okay, Mommy.' Go ahead, Mommy…you first."

Johnny's words struck a chord. I knew I was wrong in the severity of my response to my sweet son. I knew I had hurt him with my harsh words and angry tone. I could feel the eyes of my children watching me. More significantly, I could feel the eyes of heaven watching me. I laid my head down on the steering wheel and grieved over the loss of our terrific morning.

It took me a minute to say anything, but the words finally came.

"David, I know the spills were an accident and you didn't mean to drop the ice cream. I'm sorry I got so angry. Will you forgive me?"

Johnny spoke up before his brother had a chance. "David, say, 'Yes, Mommy, I forgive you.'"

David said, "Yes, Mommy, I forgive you."

"I love you, David."

"I love you too, Mommy."

As I got on the highway, I began to think about how my bossy little Johnny negotiated this peace. I felt better and I could tell by the way David was eating his sundae that he did too. It was still a terrific morning, and as I thanked God, He reminded me of something important from His Word that I needed to share with Johnny.

"Johnny, did you know that the Bible says you are blessed if you are a peacemaker and that you are called a son of God?"

"I'm a son of God?" Johnny asked, bewildered. "Like Jesus?"

"Yes. Jesus said in Matthew 5, 'Blessed are the peacemakers, for they will be called sons of God.' So when you bring peace and help people, you are being like Jesus."

Johnny was silent as he thought about this for a while, and then he said, "Hercules is the son of Zeus, but I am a son of God!" He seemed pretty pleased by the comparison.

Then he said, "If I am a son of God, I think Daddy should know about this!"

*W*endy Arneson lives in the St. Louis area with her husband, Erik, and their sons David (six), Jonathan (four), and Samuel (two). She is a full-time homemaker and enjoys reading, writing, working out, and warming benches at Little League games.

Muddling Through Mistakes and Mishaps

31

Who's in Charge?

by Kendra Smiley

oney, hop into your car seat and I'll buckle you up."

"No! I don't want to sit in my seat! I don't want to wear a seat belt! I don't want to go for a ride!"

Now what? What's a parent to do when their request is denied? What's next when the order is turned down by a four-year-old as though it were an option? What should you do if the command to "hop into your car seat" turns into WW III with your preschooler protesting loudly, kicking furiously, and swinging like a professional boxer? *Now what?*

Scenarios like this happen every day. Sometimes the disobedience or threatened disobedience is subtle…"I don't want to get in my seat," the youngster said calmly. "I'm tired. Do we have to go to the store today? Could we go tomorrow?" Sometimes it is radical…"I hate my car seat," shrieked the toddler. "I hate this car! I hate *you!*"

No one wants to have their parental authority questioned. When your child's challenge is a mild one, it is upsetting. When the response is extreme, it can be devastating. You think you are failing. Your household has been turned upside down, and you feel you are the worst parent in the entire world. Those thoughts are very real, but they are not accurate. The question is not "Who is the worst parent in the entire world?" (I'd hate to judge *that* contest.) The question is…*"Now what?"*

"I am the parent. He is the child." I said those two sentences more than once as we were raising our kids. Who was I trying to convince? Probably both of us—myself and my child. Actually, it was more of a reminder…a reminder I needed when there had been a mysterious role reversal. Saying "I am the parent…He is the child…" helped me restore each one of us to our proper place.

"I am the parent." Sounds simple, doesn't it? Of course I'm the parent. Obviously I'm the parent. I'm older. I'm wiser. I pay the bills. I make the decisions. I'm the one who is in charge. Well, er, ah, maybe not *all* the time. In fact, my recollection is that the two sentences quoted above were uttered because I had momentarily abdicated the throne and was no longer in charge (or at least things were moving in the wrong direction). Somehow my little sweetie, the cunning little toddler, the charming grade school boy, was taking control. Granted, he was neither qualified nor chosen to be in command, but evidently he had forgotten that "He was the child" and that "I was the parent." And I guess I had forgotten it too! I was in the same position as the parent with the car seat protestor. An order was given and was being debated. The parent's authority was in question.

"We have a problem in our home," the young father began as he was handed the microphone. We had just finished a strong-willed child seminar and had opened it up for questions. "Our four-year-old is running the house. What can we do?" That was it. This dear man was obviously at the end of his rope and the knot he was clinging to was fraying. His authority had been usurped by a very strong-willed child.

The honesty of that father must be appreciated and applauded. In the auditorium heads nodded in affirmation, agreement, and commiseration. The confusion of the roles of parent and child is not unusual. After having addressed thousands of parents and answering numerous questions in seminars, workshops, and via e-mail, I can attest to the fact that role reversal is a common problem.

So what is the answer?

Precisely what we heard from that father…admit that there is a problem in need of a solution. Admitting that a problem exists may appear very simple. Simple, yes…easy, not necessarily. For many, this step is extremely difficult. It seems to be easier to ignore the situation, hoping that "with time things will change." Yes, things will change with time, but if you have compromised your role as the parent, the change will not be very pleasant.

The father we heard from at the seminar was willing to acknowledge that somehow, somewhere, for whatever reason, he was no longer functioning as the parent, as the one in charge. Perhaps that is the case in your home. Maybe you are tired or under stress in another aspect of your life. Sleep deprivation is one very prevalent stressor for parents. Maybe you are a little defensive or overprotective when it comes to parenting. Maybe, for whatever reason, you feel inadequate. The car seat protestor we met felt self-assured enough to oppose his parent's order. Evidently there was confusion in their family about who was the parent and who was in charge. Admit the problem exists. Now is not the time to make excuses. Instead it is time for the truth. What is the truth for you?[3]

*K*endra and her husband, John, a retired Air Force Reserve pilot, live on a working farm in East Central Illinois. They raised three sons on that farm and now author books and speak together. Kendra's latest book is *Do Your Kids a Favor—Love Your Spouse.* Kendra hosts a daily radio program, *Live Life Intentionally,* and speaks nationally and internationally.

32

My Plan Hits Reality

by Jessica Gramm

It was Saturday night and that meant bathtime and bedtime for my two young children. My husband, Joel, a firefighter, was on shift, and I was exhausted with being newly pregnant and running around after two kids all day. My daughter, Josie, who was five at the time, had been taking gymnastics for two years, and that night a competition was on television. "If we can get done with baths and get Josiah to bed, we can snuggle and watch the gymnasts for a little while," I whispered conspiratorially.

We finished baths and I hurriedly dried off the kids. "Just let Mommy get ready for bed too," I stated. "Get on your pj's and I'll be done pretty soon." As I began my routine, Josie and Josiah began running and chasing each other in the hallway.

"Ruff, ruff," three-year-old Josiah would bark.

Josie would squeal and shout, "You can't catch me!"

"Guys, knock it off and get on your pajamas," I shouted to no avail. The game of chase was in full swing. "Somebody's going to get hurt," I cautioned in typical Mommy form. It was as if I were speaking Japanese for all the good it did. I began washing my face and then IT happened.

I heard a resounding THUMP and then the inevitable wail of pain as Josie shouted, "Mom, Josiah fell!" I was drying my face as I turned to the hallway. Reprimanding words of, "I told you someone was going to get hurt," formed and faded away as Josiah looked up at me with a gigantic gash on his forehead bubbling with dark blood.

"Oh my gosh!" I shrieked as I quickly filled my towel with cold water and pressed it against his forehead. Josie, realizing Josiah was hurt badly, began to scream. Then I did the unthinkable. "Didn't I tell you to quit running? Didn't I tell you someone would get hurt? You are the big sister, Josie. I depend on you to obey and now look what happened!" My tone was dripping with accusation. Even now as I write this, I still feel the burn of shame on my cheeks for my inappropriate response.

"I'm sorry. Oh, Josiah. Oh, Josiah. I'm so sorry," Josie wept.

I grabbed the phone and dialed my parents. No answer. I dialed my husband's parents and his sister Christa answered. She hurried over. Needing to unlock the door for her, I left Josie pressing the towel to Josiah's head. As we raced back up the stairs, we heard increased wailing, but when we arrived, it was not Josiah, but rather Josie still lamenting her brother's injuries. Josiah was very quiet with big eyes that revealed he knew that this was no normal ouchie.

"It's all my fault. It's all my fault," Josie continued to sob. Christa began reassuring her that it was not her fault, and I mumbled words in agreement still frustrated with Josie, but even more with myself. Whose fault was it, really? Was it anyone's fault at all? If fault was to be found, it certainly did not belong to a five-year-old girl who was just playing chase, even if she was disobeying. If anything, the blame was mine. Why didn't I wait until later to tend to my own needs? Why didn't I step into the hallway and physically stop them from running?

We loaded up and headed for the hospital. I reached my parents on their cell and met them on the road to receive a highly distraught Josie. Upon arriving at the ER, we were immediately ushered back to a room. "How did this happen?" was a question I answered repeatedly.

"Well, they were playing puppy chase and he fell and hit his head on the corner of the wall."

"Ah yes, the corner will do it every time," was the response most often given.

Josiah's gash was more than an inch long and about a centimeter wide. His head split clear to the skull bone, which actually had a visible dent in it. My brave little man did not cry at all. He only whimpered slightly when they gave the numbing injections. We had a plastic surgeon called in since the wound was so large and centered on his forehead. He stitched eight layers of skin with 10 stitches per layer, leaving us with a whopping 80-stitch head injury. Josiah fell asleep during the stitching.

We arrived home close to midnight. Exhausted, I fell into bed with Josiah next to me.

The next morning we eagerly awaited Daddy's return. We attended church as a family, and I went through the day in emotional turmoil. I blamed myself repeatedly and felt that I had failed as a mother not just to Josiah, but perhaps more so to Josie.

Later when I apologized to Josie, she just smiled in the sweet way that little girls do. "It's okay, Mama. I should have obeyed. I love you. You're the best Mom in the whole world." And with that, she threw her arms around me. It was such simple and free-flowing forgiveness. The kind our Father in heaven offers us when we mess up. The kind we need to offer each other—especially when we don't have a relaxing evening the way we planned.

Jessica Gramm has been the wife to Joel for ten wonderful years. They have three beautiful children: Josie (seven), Josiah (four), and Jude (one). Jessica is blessed to be a stay-at-home mom; it is her calling and passion in life. She is thankful to be saved by grace and reminded each day of God's great mercy.

33

Shots and Spots

by Cyndie Claypool de Neve

I have a confession. I sent my son to school with chicken pox.

I know, I know. Parents curse others who send their kids to school with fevers and viruses, which are shared so generously from one child to the next.

But the chicken pox? Now that's the granddaddy of all no-nos. That means sending the classmate home with germs that mandate isolation for a week or more.

How could I do such a miserable thing?

Well, here I have to plead ignorance.

I, like every parent I've talked to since my son's diagnosis, wrongly assumed that having my child vaccinated against chicken pox meant that he could never get chicken pox.

So when a white spot appeared in his mouth, I dismissed it as a cold sore. When he complained about a bump on his head, I assumed he had bonked his noggin. I also rationalized away his nausea and glassy eyes.

When he came downstairs the next morning complaining about spots on his face, did I even then realize he had chicken pox?

Nope. I declared them hives and gave him antihistamine.

Funny thing, though. Those little white spots didn't go away. They doubled faster than a marshmallow in the microwave. That ruled out early onset pimples as well as a family of spiders who might have feasted on his lightly toasted skin.

Stumped, I looked through my medical book of nasty illnesses and gross health conditions.

Chicken pox? Couldn't be that, I was certain. He'd been vaccinated. But there was a simple test. Check the upper trunk area, where chicken pox usually starts.

My children, ages five and nine at the time, were quite amused to learn they have "trunks." After a litany of "nos"—no, it's not like a tree's trunk, or a storage trunk, or an elephant's trunk, and no, they don't mean the "swimming trunks area"—I wished I hadn't read that sentence out loud and simply asked him to lift his shirt.

I also wished I had started the morning with coffee, especially since now I had to answer the perplexing question about why we call our torso our trunk while an elephant's trunk is his nose.

As I pretended to know what I was talking about, I lifted my son's shirt to discover 20 spots on his back alone. But I still wasn't convinced. After all, every medical book and website I fumbled through that morning described chicken pox as red spots or a rash. What the information neglected to explain was that chicken pox starts out as a splattering of white, scattered spots.

By the time I got hold of the pediatrician's office, his spots had doubled again.

"Could my son have chicken pox even if he has been vaccinated?" I asked.

The nurse didn't stop to think, didn't consult medical journals, didn't ask the doctor. She replied quite confidently, "Yes."

Not exactly the answer I was hoping for.

The doctor was just as decisive with his diagnosis. Turns out, there's even a special name for it, "breakthrough chicken pox," which can occur in up to 30 percent of vaccinated children, according to the American Academy of Pediatrics. The benefit to the vaccine is that these "breakthrough" varieties are supposed to be mild with fewer complications.

My son's, however, was far from mild. He ended up with nearly 200 spots, and he generously gave them to at least two others, including his sister.

My daughter's case was so mild, fewer than 20 spots with most on her chest and legs, that I easily could have written off the random white (not red) spots on her face as, well, pretty much anything else. Her other symptom was a sudden desire to take afternoon naps—not exactly something I'd complain about.

The day my son was able to return to school, he brought home a flier warning about possible exposure to chicken pox. "A little late," he joked as he handed it to me.

The other mothers from the class had comforted themselves knowing their children had been vaccinated.

Until I told them—so had mine.

yndie Claypool de Neve is a freelance writer who lives in Escondido, California, with her husband, Marcel, and their two children, Elliott and Zoe. She writes a newspaper column about family life and is the communications specialist for Moms in Touch International, a global prayer ministry.

34

Wake-Up Call

by Mary Steinke

I think I hurt the baby!" I cried to my husband the night we brought our firstborn home from the hospital.

"What's wrong?" Harry groaned as he tried to wake himself up.

What was wrong was the fact I had a new baby and didn't know what in heaven I was doing. I felt completely clueless.

Around midnight I had gotten up to nurse the baby for the first time at night in our home. The infant's cries woke the dog, who whimpered to go outside at the same time our infant cried as though his lungs would burst. Since I didn't want a doggie accident on the kitchen tile, I decided that baby Brian could wait 30 seconds while I let the dog out. I recognized the dog's whimper well enough to know that the lovable family mutt couldn't wait at all.

To put the dog outside, I needed both hands free to hook the dog's collar to a chain. Carefully, I laid our newborn down on the couch on his back as I'd seen 50 other competent moms do. What I didn't realize was that our couch wasn't designed like the couches of the 50 other competent moms who safely laid their infants on their sofas. Our sofa was sloped with a rounded edge, not completely flat with squared-off edges.

Brian quickly escalated from irritated crying to furious bellowing as he waited for his predawn snack. He flailed his arms so much as he cried that he began to rock back and forth toward the slope of the sofa. From five feet away and much too far to reach him in time, I helplessly watched as my three-day-old infant rolled off the couch and fell almost two feet to the carpeted floor.

Instantly, I scooped him up, darted to the bedroom, and woke up my husband with tears streaming down my cheeks. Our son wouldn't stop screaming. I couldn't stop shaking. This wasn't at all how I pictured our first night at home together.

After we checked the baby's limbs and head for any obvious injuries, Harry suggested that he call our pediatrician while I tried to feed Brian to calm him down. Once the baby started to eat and quieted himself, I stopped shaking on the outside. I was still shaking on the inside. The little confidence I once had in myself as a mother was now completely gone. On the phone, our doctor determined that since our newborn remained calm, nursed well, and showed no obvious signs of injuries that he would see us in his office the first thing in the morning instead of sending us to the ER.

All I could think about were worst case scenarios. What if I caused irreparable damage to my baby? Would the State take custody of my son due to my neglect? What if Brian screamed in fear every time I came near him? Could my husband ever trust me to take care of our son again? Would I ever learn to trust myself as a mother? What if even *one* of my wild imaginings came true? In my own mind, I was already a failure as a mom before I ever really had the chance to succeed.

The rest of the night I spent curled up next to my newborn on a quilt on the floor with my hand on his chest to make sure he was still breathing while I stayed awake with my questions until dawn. I prayed that somehow, something good would come from my momentary error in judgment.

The next morning Brian seemed just fine—hungry, alert, and ready for a new day. I, on the other hand, wasn't ready to face the doctor.

Our pediatrician gave him a thorough exam, asked lots of questions, and put us at ease. He told us in his 20 years of practice he had seen far worse falls happen to newborns with no long-term effects. However, he wanted to see the baby again at the end of the week, gave us a list of potential physical and developmental symptoms to look for down the road, and told us not to worry. But worry we did.

During the weeks that followed what we lovingly refer to as "The Night Baby Brian Took a Header," I discovered that the only place to go from my ineptitude as an inexperienced mom was, frankly, up.

Today, Brian directs his own plays, films his own movies, and writes his own novels that he hopes to publish after college graduation. With no physical, emotional, or mental challenges from that infamous fall off the sloped sofa, he still loves his parents in spite of our rocky start. He also mostly loves his two younger siblings, who *didn't* fall off the sofa as newborns.

Back then, no one could have convinced me that I would ever be a good mom.

Yet in my failure as a brand-new mother, I found a brand-new side of God. The night Brian fell, I fell on the mercy of God. As I comforted my baby during that long night, God comforted me.

Brian falling on his first night home was the wake-up call I needed to understand that I can *never* do this mothering thing alone. I needed Someone stronger than my own shortcomings. I needed to understand that when my child falls down in my care or in his choices in life, God sees. I needed to know that regardless of my many mistakes, mess ups, or missteps as a mom, God forgives me. I needed to believe that when I fall short every day as a mother, God still loves me.

For no matter what falls in and into my life, God is always bigger. He loves to comfort mothers, mistakes and all.

Mary writes a column, devotionals, magazine, and online newsletter articles, speaks at retreats and moms groups, serves as a discussion leader for Bible Study Fellowship, and has served at Hearts at Home for many years. Mary resides in Normal, Illinois, with her husband, Harry, and three sons.

35

The Perfect Corsage

by Connie Pombo

"Mom, did you pick up Justine's corsage?"
"No, honey. I thought you did."

"Moothhherrrrr…the prom is in three hours! Can you puhleeeeze pick it up?"

As a mother of two sons, I've been relegated the honor of "picking out" and "picking up" corsages for my sons' dates for the last eight years. This was the final prom corsage.

After nearly a decade of "prom duty," I knew the importance of details—especially corsages. But for some reason a "prom cloud" hovered over us—something *always* went wrong at the last minute.

With prior corsage nightmares still lingering in my head, I jumped in the car and prayed, "Please let this be the perfect corsage."

When I arrived at the florist, there were three moms ahead of me—picking up their sons' corsages. As each one made their debut from the display case, we oohed and ahhed. I felt hopeful that this time would be different.

As I slipped to the front of the line, the florist with crinkling eyes smiled and said, "Name, please."

"Jonathan Pombo," I said with a grin.

I was almost giddy with excitement—as if it were my prom—until she laid the corsage box on the counter.

No, not again. It can't be!

The corsage was a spring mix of red and yellow flowers (I had ordered pink). To make matters worse, it was a pin-on corsage—not a wristlet (Justine's dress was strapless). And then there was the box—it was huge—almost coffinlike. The tiny corsage lay lifeless in a bed of fluorescent cellophane shreds.

A lump formed in my throat as I whimpered, "Excuse me, but I think this is the *wrong* corsage."

The florist removed the pencil from behind her ear and checked the order sheet. "No, it says 'Pombo'—there's no mistake."

I stopped cringing long enough to take a closer look. *Maybe if it was in a smaller box, it wouldn't look so pitiful.*

As the florist rang up my purchase, I offered a suggestion. "Do you happen to have a smaller box?"

"Absolutely not," she countered. "We're completely out of corsage boxes."

I reluctantly paid for the corsage and carried it to the car with a heavy heart. I needed to call my son.

"Jon, there's a little problem."

"Mom—it's okay—just come home!"

When I drove up our long driveway, I was greeted by Jon at the side entrance.

"So what do you think?" I sniffled.

"I think it needs a smaller box?"

I burst into tears. "No, not again. Can't it be perfect just once?"

My mind raced—I had two hours left! I could try the family-owned florist down the street.

"Jon, keep the corsage in the refrigerator until I get back," I shouted.

As I entered the small one-room florist shop, the door made a jingle and the scent of roses wafted through the air.

"Excuse me, I'm in a hurry," I stammered. "Do you have any prom corsages?"

The florist glared at me and snapped, "No, we closed five minutes ago!"

Back in the car, I called Jon while I fought back tears. "I'm driving downtown—keep the corsage cool."

"Mom, there's not enough time—"

"Don't wait for me. I'll meet you at the church for pictures. I promise."

I threaded my way through traffic and practiced my opening line, "HELP ME!"

I swerved into the parking lot of the *third* florist—armed with a picture of Justine's dress.

As I approached the counter my voice trembled, "I need a pink corsage and you're my last hope."

Apologetically, the florist explained, "We're out of pink flowers. But someone just returned a corsage—it's in the display case. It might be what you're looking for."

I thanked her as I rounded the corner. There were green buckets of white carnations and daisies, but nothing in pink. And then out of the corner of my eye—on the top shelf—a corsage box.

My heart pounded heavily as I reached for the box. To my delight, it was a wristlet corsage made up of seven sweetheart roses in pale pink. There was a ribbon of pearls, a sprig of baby's breath, and holly fern. It was perfect!

I glanced at my watch—20 minutes to get to the church. I paid for the corsage and scampered out the door.

As I drove into the parking lot, I saw an ocean of limos and a sea of tuxes. *How will I ever find Jon?*

Then he appeared out of nowhere. The picture of the once little boy—now a man with strong shoulders, standing tall and handsome—made me fight back tears. His boutonnière clumsily hung sideways as he reached out to hug me. I inwardly smiled, reveling in the moment.

"Mom, did you find it? I brought the other one just in case."

"There's no need, honey. Look at what I have."

Jon's green eyes sparkled with excitement. "Thanks, Mom!"

We walked to the reflecting pool where the formal pictures were being taken. Justine looked like a princess, and together they looked like the top of a wedding cake.

I looked on expectantly as Jon placed the corsage on Justine's wrist while I snapped the picture of a lifetime. She was smiling into his eyes and gasped, "Jon, it's absolutely perfect!"

With misty eyes I followed them out to the limo and stood waving until they disappeared out of sight.

I stayed up for Jon's return that night. It was a little past midnight when I heard the door close softly. I crept off the sofa and asked, "Jon, how was the prom?"

"It was okay. The dinner was cold, the room was hot, but Justine loved her corsage!"

With a twinkle in his eye, he added, "Thanks, Mom. You did it again."

"No, Jon, God did it. He always works things out perfectly when we leave them in His hands."

onnie Pombo is an inspirational speaker, author, and founder of Women's Mentoring Ministries in Mt. Joy, Pennsylvania. When not speaking or writing, Connie enjoys spending time with her husband of 31 years, and their two sons: Jeremy (26) and Jonathan (21). She can be reached at www.conniepombo.com.

36

Sledding into Hope

by Tena DeGraaf

Newly fallen snow beckoned our family to come outside. My husband, Steve, and I answered the call and decided to take our boys, Daniel and Mitchell, out to sled at Steve's parents' cottage on Lake Petenwell in Wisconsin. Steve, who stated he would be out in a minute, was still visiting with his mom and dad as I headed out with the boys. The cottage has a walkout basement with sliding glass doors that lead to the lake. On each side of the back of the house, there are two small hills that slope down to the grass that touches the back patio. Daniel, age four, began to take his sled to the top of the one hill and slide down gleefully. I was so proud of him! He had never been sledding, and I was impressed with his ability. Mitch, on the other hand, at age three looked like the abominable snowman. He could not move in his snowsuit. He stood still with his arms and legs straddled. I plopped him down on his sled, and I remember very distinctly thinking, *What a wonderful family day; I am going to push Mitch as hard as I can!*

As soon as I let go of Mitch's sled, I knew exactly what I had done wrong. I am left-handed, and I had pushed much harder with my left hand than my right hand. Instead of remaining parallel with the lake and the cottage as his brother had so expertly demonstrated, Mitch veered for the lake, gaining momentum with each inch. Now, what I did not mention earlier about the landscape is the fact that the back-yard declines to an edge. Between the grass and the lake is an eight foot drop with a border of huge rocks and boulders that the lake water laps up against when it melts.

Immediately, I began to race as best I could, which was not very fast because I had on my snowmobile suit and boots. My boys are only 14½ months apart, and when Mitch was a baby, Daniel could not say Mitch but could call him Meme. To this day our family members still call him Meme. As I ran to try to catch Mitch, I yelled, "Hang on, Meme! Hang on!" His father, who had witnessed this event from the basement, began sprinting and shouting at me to get Mitch, which was physically impossible. Together we watched our baby (three-year-olds are babies when they are in trouble) fly 30 feet in the air and land on the ice with the sled firmly attached to his bottom.

We rushed to grab hold of him and examined him for any cuts, bruises, and broken bones. Miraculously, he was fine. After checking Mitch over thoroughly, Steve took him inside the cottage. I grabbed the sled. I felt like the worst mom in the world. What I had intended to be a fun family day had ended abruptly because I had made a ter-rible mistake that could have truly wounded my son. I have had many years to replay this event in my mind, and each time I think about it, one feeling overwhelms me. It is the word "crummy." I felt as though I was the crummiest mom in the world, but as I climbed the rocks with the sled on my back and tears streaming down my face, two thoughts gave me a glimmer of hope.

The first thought was the fact that God had spared Mitch's life and had kept him from harm. The other thought was what Daniel had yelled to Mitch. My husband and I offered no sound advice. I had yelled, "Hang on, Meme! Hang on!" That was the worst recom-mendation! Moms, if you are ever in a situation where your child is sledding down a hill heading for disaster, DO NOT, I repeat, DO NOT yell "HANG ON!" Had I been thinking more clearly, I should have yelled, "Roll off, Meme! Roll off!" Bless his three-year-old heart; he obeyed his mother and hung on for dear life! His father was too busy trying to tell me to grab him, which was unattainable at that point. However, his brother at four years old knew the encouragement Mitch needed to hear. Amidst the shouting of his parents, Dan stood at the top of the hill and yelled at the top of his lungs, "Don't worry, Meme! Jesus is with you!"

Somehow between his home life, Sunday school, and MOPS, Dan had hidden this message of hope in his heart, and he was able to proclaim it to his little brother at the exact moment of need. Those words not only gave Mitchie the encouragement he needed, but Dan's words gave me hope that even though I make mistakes as a mom, God is still working in the lives of my children.

ena DeGraaf is a writer, speaker, and educator. She and her husband of 13 years, Stephen, are the parents of Daniel (11), and Mitchell (10). She loves spending time with her family. Together, they bike ride often. She enjoys watching her boys' soccer, basketball, and baseball games.

God-Touches in the Trenches

37

A Parent Too

by Cheri Keaggy

It was my first pregnancy. My belly was steadily growing along with the excitement and wonder of becoming a new mom. My husband and I had baby names already picked out. If it was a girl, we'd name her Sarah, a biblical name which means "princess." If it was a boy, it would be Cameron, which means, well, "crooked nose." We were thrilled to be adding a new member to our family. Like a sponge, I absorbed everything I could get my hands on about pregnancy and parenting. Though this was new territory, I was gung ho to learn as much as possible about taking care of a new baby. I had decided my child would have nothing but the best, including a brand-new oak-finish crib, a trendy aqua-colored stroller, and the time-tested cloth diaper.

My husband was running a successful sound company at the time while I held an office job at a local printing company. I wasn't making a ton of money, but as a young married couple, we had bought a new house, so every little bit helped. Although all I ever wanted to do was be a wife and a mom, I assumed that after the baby came I would have to return to work to continue supplementing our income. But, the further along I got in my pregnancy, the more I dreaded the thought of sending my precious baby off to day care.

I remember the day it hit me the hardest. I was at work typing reports and answering phones when the topic of my maternity leave came up. Somehow I had been under the impression that I would be afforded six months at home with my new baby. However, I had grossly misunderstood. My heart sank when I learned it was six *weeks*, not six months. I was devastated. With emotions spinning, I quickly paid a visit to the human resources office in hopes of hearing a different report.

There on the couch I cried my eyes out to a kind woman named Becky. She, too, was a mom. She listened patiently as I shared how *I* wanted to be the one to hear my baby's first words and to see his first steps. *I* wanted to be the one to comfort him when he cries and to discover what makes him giggle. *I* wanted to be able to nurse him and rock him to sleep. In short, I was selfish. But it was the good kind of selfishness, the kind every mother should be allowed to feel. I simply didn't want to share those special moments with anyone else. I had already fallen in love. While the little person taking shape inside of me had slowly secured a place in my belly, he was now securing a place in my heart. Becky was as sweet and understanding as she could be, but no amount of tears could change company policy. It was time to have a talk with my husband.

Through more tears and a loving embrace, the decision was made. I would not return to work once the baby was born. We weren't quite sure how we would do it, but we felt somehow that God would honor our decision. While we had a little money saved up in the bank, this was definitely a step of faith. Still, God had blessed us with this child, and we wanted to be the ones to raise it.

During this time I had been helping out with music at church, mostly playing the keyboard on Sunday mornings. We hadn't told anyone of our decision because I intended to keep working as long as my swollen ankles would let me. No one knew except God. And He was busy unfolding a plan.

As best as I can recall, my husband and I had made our decision on a Thursday. Surprisingly, that very next Sunday the pastor pulled my husband aside to see if I'd be interested in a job at the church. He said the part-time position of worship coordinator wouldn't pay much, but I could do most of the work at home and come in once a week for a planning meeting. The pastor had no idea that just a few days prior we had determined I would stay home once the baby came, even though we knew it would stretch us financially. We took it as a direct provision from heaven when we learned that my starting salary would be the exact amount I was making at my 40-hour-a-week job!

We were amazed. We had stepped out in faith and God had provided. Not only would I be the primary caregiver of my baby, I would be able to continue my involvement with worship at church. Funny thing is, I was already fully committed to helping out with the music ministry, and now they were going to pay me for it! Clearly, God was in control.

On an October day, Cameron Keaggy was born. I still remember the sound of his first cry and the instinct I had to count his fingers and toes just to make sure they were all there. I remember the sense of wonder I felt over this incredible gift God had given us. And the cloth diapers, well...that lasted about a week before we made the switch to disposables. Desperate times call for desperate measures...and a few modern conveniences.

Proud as any parents who ever lived, we couldn't wait to show our baby boy off that first Sunday back at church. It was there that I would later write my very first worship song followed by a ballad for Cameron called "Little Boy on His Knees." Both songs would be recorded on my debut album, *Child of the Father*. And, to our great joy, Sarah Lindsay Keaggy was born in November, two years later, just as God would have it.

Does God have a plan for your life? Could it be that He has your best interests at heart? You bet. After all, God's a Parent too.

*S*inger/songwriter Cheri Keaggy makes her home in Nashville, Tennessee, with her husband, Eddie, and their two beautiful children, Cameron (18) and Sarah (16). She enjoys walking her Shih Tzu, cleaning the house, hanging with friends, playing Ms. Pacman, and studying God's Word. Visit www.cherikeaggy.com to read her latest blog.

38

At the Wheel

by Amy Young

I am a cautious person and, by extension, a cautious mother. You won't find my children on skateboards, riding bikes without helmets, crossing streets without *at least* one responsible adult, or eating sloppy joes with any less than three napkins on their laps. It is my job to keep my girls, Isabel (eight) and Sophie (seven), safe and clean, and I take that job very seriously. Over time, however, I have realized there is a problem with my approach to safety. You see, cautious mothers raise cautious children. That seems like a good thing, right? Yes. Caution is good for public safety, but not necessarily good for finding your way in this big, crazy world. I know from experience. I wonder how my children will discover themselves, learn forgiveness, love deeply, or know God without taking a few risks. So, my favorite memory involves a moment when I decided to take a small risk, and my girls went along for the ride. Literally.

Each summer our family spends a month at a family cabin on a lake in Minnesota. My husband, Greg, grew up skiing and fishing there with his grandfather, eating the homemade bread and rhubarb pies his grandmother served. Now, on weekends my father-in-law drives the boat and Greg skis. The girls ride the Jet Ski, swim with cousins, and jump off the boat into the crystal clear water of the spring-fed lake. I like to sit on the dock with a hat and a good book and watch all of the action. Unfortunately, during the week, when my father-in-law goes home to work, there is no one to pull my husband on skis. Greg pulls the girls on the tube and takes us out for trolling lunches and sunset cruises, but no skiing for him. He has begged me to learn. I have firmly declined. It just isn't safe with me at the helm.

Last summer, I began to think. My girls are watching, and I can do this. I can help my husband and show my girls what it means to try new things. I decided I would learn to drive a boat and pull my husband on skis that summer. "Waaaiiiiit…" my anxious mind protested, "what if the boat crashes, he hits his head, the wind picks up, the lake gets too busy, I can't see, I miss the gear shift, the brakes stop working, I get scared…?" But when I saw the excited and determined look on my husband's face, I knew I was going to do it anyway. And over the next week, under his patient tutelage, I learned to pull him 500 yards in a straight line without another soul on the lake. Mission accomplished, right?

And then the last day of our vacation arrived. We were packing up and taking a last look around. The lake was liquid sterling under cool, cottony skies. There wasn't even a whisper of wind. It was a perfect morning for a ski. My husband looked at me longingly. My girls looked at me longingly. How could I say no? So, in the gray air of that August morning, we emerged on the dock in our swimsuits and sweatshirts, the birds talking back to us in their morning twitter. Isabel would be the spotter. "Now," I said, "you can't take your eyes off your dad, right?" "Right, Mommy," she said. Sophie would guard the dog, Napoleon, and watch for passenger boats. "You have to yell loud if you see a boat, right, Sophie?" "Right, Mommy," she said. I would be in charge of the boat. Gulp.

With these roles assigned and Dad bobbing in the lake behind us, my girls and I navigated the boat out of its slip. Isabel threw the rope to her father. Sophie watched for reeds and talked me through the narrow channel out into the open water. I gently moved the throttle forward, stretching the rope taut and waiting nervously for my husband to get set. Suddenly, Greg yelled, "Hit it!" Isabel echoed, "Hit it!" And we were off. Miraculously, physics took over and Greg popped out of the water, cutting beautifully across the wake like a knife through liquid glass. The girls screamed, "He's up!" and "Yaaay, Mommy!" as we slid through the luscious velvet morning. Isabel yelled authoritatively, "Around again, Mommy," and "Too fast, Mommy," or "Too slow." Sophie chattered, calling out loon sightings and waving to early risers just emerging on their docks with steaming coffee and tousled hair. Greg whooped, his deep voice booming as he swished through the surface in iridescent arcs of spray. After 20 minutes of running smooth, error-free laps around the north end of the lake, he dropped the rope and we headed for home. In the dripping silence we docked the boat, took one last family dip, and closed our suitcases with a final, satisfied snap. Mission accomplished.

You might wonder if that moment changed me, and I overcame my ever-cautious nature. The answer is no. My girls still stay firmly within my grasp in busy parking lots, and they are *never* allowed to like boys (smile). It is the unique and privileged burden of motherhood to worry, and I know that part of me will never change. But that August moment lives in my mind like a picture-perfect snapshot in a photo album. I want to relive the feeling, and I want my girls to do the same. So I look for moments. I reach out more to others and try new things. I know that will involve some failure, and yes, some heartache for us all. But I am willing to suffer those for more moments like the one we experienced that August morning, when the conditions were just right and we drove together at full throttle, wind in our hair, joy in our voices, and God at the wheel.

*A*my Young lives in Lake Zurich, Illinois, with her husband, Greg, and their girls, Isabel (nine) and Sophie (seven). Amy enjoys running and cooking, and she always has her nose in a book. She loves being a mom because it has humbled her and retaught her the joy of laughter.

39

Kissing the Finials

by Mary DeMuth

On my run this morning, I remembered the scene from *It's a Wonderful Life* where George Bailey, now very much alive after his encounter with Clarence, runs into his home, kisses his family, and grabs the round finial to the stair banister. It comes off in his hand, still broken. With a flourish, he kisses it.

George, in that scene, embraces what is askew. He revels in the chaos with joy. He's far more concerned with his family and their love than he is about fixing up his house. After seeing what life would have been like had he not been born, George finally comes alive. And in that state, he kisses the finial.

That's a picture for me as a mom. I am an all or nothing gal. I want everything in its place before I can feel safe or relaxed. I suppose I have some medically significant disorder, one with a lot of letters, I'm sure. Even yesterday I spent a good portion of my morning organizing my kitchen because the disarray bothered me so much.

But really, I want to be a finial kisser like George. I want to be able to run into my home with joy on my face and grab my family, smothering them with affection. I want to be able to see the imperfections of my home as joy producing. A reminder that people are more important than silly things. And that I'm not living for organization or perfectly lined shelves. And that God has much to teach me when things aren't just so.

Could it be that God wants to be my safety? My rest? I'm afraid I've relied on props in my life to keep me satisfied. I've held the false belief that if all the props were in their proper place, I'd feel okay. Things like:

- All the pertinent phone numbers written on one piece of paper, instead of numbers scribbled on gum wrappers, pizza flyers, or receipts—all multiplying happily in my junk drawer.

- Children who automatically (and joyfully!) make their beds, put away their clothes, say "please" and "thank you," and brush their teeth.

- An uncluttered kitchen where food doesn't grow green hair in the fridge or the chips in the pantry aren't bendable and stale.

- A garage uncluttered with sporting goods, bikes, bits of trash, and old science experiments.

- Bathrooms with toilet lids down and no pretty rings around their bowls.

- A minivan with nary a wrapper in sight, not one seat stain, and no scrapes from parking lot mayhem.

- Laundry organized into each child's bin, folded by him or her, and put away on the day it's washed.

- Children's bedrooms that don't exponentially grow paper: homework paper, wrappers from forbidden candy, and little scraps of sentimental notes.

- The perfect family calendar, all color coded—so cleverly devised that I'd never miss a concert, a meeting with a teacher, or an appointment with the dentist.

But life is seldom all in its place like that, is it? Finials are unattached. Phone numbers are lost. Children don't always obey or clean or organize their mountains of things. The fridge doesn't toss out its moldy contents (though I wish it did). The garage stays the catch-all that it is. The bathrooms might be clean for a moment, but that moment passes much too quickly. The minivan hatches dirt and mess. The laundry never does itself. Our kids' bedrooms are *not* like Etch A Sketches, where with one hardy shake, everything magically turns to order. The calendar is only as accurate as the children who report events to Mom—a truly flawed system.

My prayer is that I'd somehow be able to take a refuge from myself, my perfectionism, my need for my world to be utterly ordered. I need God's help to kiss the finials and love my family in the chaos. It's a tricky thing to rest in disorganization. And really, the only way I can do that is to remember what George Bailey learned: family is precious and things pale in comparison. I'll add a third: God makes a house a home. He enables me to embrace my kids, messiness and all. For that, I'm grateful.

Mary DeMuth helps families turn their trials into triumphs. Her parenting books include *Ordinary Mom, Extraordinary God; Building the Christian Family You Never Had;* and *Authentic Parenting in a Postmodern Culture.* Mom to Sophie, Aidan, and Julia, Mary and her husband, Patrick, live in Texas.

40

Encounter with Wonder

by Lise Gerhard

The rain had stopped. It had cleared the Swiss air and given leaves and grass a new coat of lush green. The world outside looked refreshed, renewed, and ready to present itself at its best to whoever would take the time to admire its beauty.

I had promised my two-year-old daughter Anaïs that we would take a stroll that morning since I needed a few items from our local store. By the time we were ready, the sun was shining. When I opened the door, my daughter rushed out to unknown scents, sounds, and feelings. We hadn't walked far however when she decidedly let go of my hand and went on her own expedition, braving stones and pine cones, enemies to her unsteady toddler's feet. She finally disappeared behind a tree, leaving me unaccompanied.

Alone, I sat down on an inviting stone and watched the clouds chasing each other playfully. After some length of time and still no sign of my daughter, I started wondering if her adventures would keep her away for the whole morning. I wanted to keep to my original plan of walking to the shop, and such a delay only raised my blood pressure. I impatiently called to her several times before I heard her voice assuring me that she would be there in a minute. Another minute!

Then I heard light but determined footsteps approaching and I stood up, ready to resume our journey. Before I was able to catch a glimpse of her, though, a sharp cry pierced the air.

"Mummy, Mummy, what's *that?*" She had suddenly stopped a few yards from where I stood and was stooping over something that lay in the middle of the path.

"Come on, darling. Let's go now. We need food for lunch."

"Mummy, Mummy, come and look. What's *that?*" Upon her insistence I reluctantly stepped nearer, expecting to find another piece of grass, a stone, or maybe a dead fly. What else could be so intriguing to a toddler? Surely, *I* hadn't noticed anything when I walked the same path a few minutes ago...and neither could I see anything now. Anaïs was bent so close to the ground that I couldn't even make out the shape or the size of this unknown object. Slightly irritated, I said, "Well, then, let me have a look!"

She slowly turned toward me, eyes wide with expectation, gently inquiring one more time, "Please, Mummy, what is it?"

Surprise and slight disgust prevented me from giving her an extended answer. "Why, dear, that's only a *slug!*" What on earth was there to a small, brown, slimy slug?

"Come on now, I'd like to move on."

"But, Mummy, look, it's moving!"

At that moment, I thought it best to give up on going anywhere or doing anything as it would only stress one person: me! So I took a deep breath, calmed down, and decided to initiate my young biologist to the scarce facts I knew about slugs. I knelt down by her side and showed her how the slug could move. She was quite impressed by the antennas, not to mention the slimy trail the slug had already left behind.

We had observed the creature for some time and I was getting bored. My inner adult voice was reminding me that I still hadn't *accomplished* anything this morning:

"Shall we walk to the playground and build a sand castle?"

"Oh, but, Mummy, may I *touch* it?"

At least she wasn't a baby anymore and wasn't planning on exploring its consistency with her mouth. But still, *touch* a slug, just for the fun of it? Yuck!

Before disappointing her with an unfounded no, I settled down and made a conscious effort to see the whole story from my daughter's perspective. After listening to my many words about this extraordinary creature, she needed to experience firsthand what those words meant. After all, a slug isn't poisonous or dangerous—at the most, it's dirty.

"Yes, darling, go ahead! It won't harm you."

She very softly stroked the slug and then gently pushed it, observing its reaction. Satisfied at last, she jumped up and ran away to yet new discoveries.

Now I was the one who stayed behind, pondering our morning encounter. What about me? Was I as enthusiastic about God's creation as my daughter was? Was I ready to put aside to-do lists, plans, and programs, to take the time to share God's amazing creativity and power with my loved ones? Since that morning, my heart holds a small "slug light," and it blinks, now and then, reminding me to slow down, wonder, and praise our Creator.

*L*ise and her husband, Bilal, are the grateful parents of two girls, Anaïs (three) and Noélia (eighteen months). She never thought mothering would be so beautiful and challenging and enjoys it greatly (except at night...). She also loves singing for friends, family, or just herself at their home in Switzerland.

41

I Don't Like You, Mommy

by Danielle E. Crowell

don't like you, Mommy. I like Daddy better," were the words launched out of the mouth of my two-year-old daughter. She said this straight-faced, not once, but three times in a row as she was finishing *my* bowl of soup. Knowing my strong-willed child was once again testing me for a reaction, I tried to think of an appropriate response. For a fleeting moment my thoughts screamed: *You little stinker—you have no idea how hard I work for you. Do you realize I quit my job to stay home with you. I have a master's degree, and all I do is wait on you hand and foot.*

But after an awkward silence, I managed to reply, "Well, honey, I love *you* very much." Then I calmly walked to the kitchen sink to break, I mean, finish the dishes. The last thing I wanted to do was overreact or say the wrong thing. Logically, I knew she said this to test my reaction and see how far she could push me. She "doesn't like me" right now because she spends most of her time with me. While Daddy is at work, I am the main enforcer of our house rules. She sees me as the policewoman. But despite these reasons, her words still stung. *This has to be a teachable moment,* I thought. *I just don't know what to teach...*

"I don't like you," is even worse than the greeting I received earlier in the week when I went to get her out of bed. I walked in with a smile, asked what she wanted for breakfast, and the first thing the cherub said to me was, "Daddy. I want my daddy. Where'd my daddy go?"

Or even last week when we spent the day singing, baking, playing, painting, potty training, and basically trashing the house. The second Daddy walked in from work, I didn't exist. "Daddy, oh Daddy! I love you so much, Daddy!" as she raced into his arms. She has yet to voluntarily say those words to me.

But tonight tops it all. She actually verbalized one of my greatest fears, "I don't like you, Mommy. I like Daddy better." Ouch. I would give my life for this child. And she tells me she doesn't like me?

It was a teachable moment all right, but more for me than for her. She was just trying out a new phrase. But I was beginning to learn what God's unconditional love is all about.

Later that night I realized that perhaps God let this happen so that I could begin to understand His love for me. Growing up and even recently, I secretly doubted that God loved me as much as others. I mean, how could He know all of my thoughts and deeds and still love me? I understood how He could love others, but not me.

Now that I am a mom, I am starting to get His unconditional love. Just as God sees me all the time, I witness my daughter's behavior every waking moment: the good, the bad, and the ugly. Yet I love her. I love her no more or no less when she warms my heart or when she breaks it. Even in the midst of her thoughtless words, there is absolutely nothing my daughter could say or do that would cause me to stop loving her. If she were to commit the worst crime ever, I would be absolutely devastated, but I would not stop loving her. This is how God loves me. This is how God loves you!

After years of struggling to understand how God could love me unconditionally, He is teaching me about His love through my own daughter. I am so thankful for the gift of being a parent and for the sacred glimpse it has given me into God's loving heart. By His grace, I will continue to assure my daughter of my unconditional love for her—especially when she says, "I don't like you, Mommy. I like Daddy better." And this will help me to remember that God loves me, even when I act like I don't like Him.

*D*anielle Crowell lives in Metamora, Illinois, with her dear sleep-deprived husband, T.J., and two vivacious daughters, Grace (three) and Caroline (two). Danielle and T.J. are expecting their third child in February 2008. She is active in her church's moms group, speaks at local moms groups, and participates in a weekly radio program for moms in Central Illinois. She loves being a mom because it keeps her humble and dependent upon the grace, strength, and wisdom of God—every moment, every day.

42

Busyness and Big Bird

by Crystal Bowman

As busy mothers know, it's hard to squeeze in time for yourself. The needs of a growing family are so intense and demanding that personal time becomes a precious commodity. I was thrilled when I had the rare opportunity to make it through a shower without interruption or use the bathroom without an audience. What was even more challenging was squeezing in time alone with God. Some call this experience their "quiet time"; others call it "personal devotions." Whatever you want to call it, it's difficult to fit this spiritual practice into an already overbooked schedule.

When my three children were beyond potty training age and nighttime feedings, I was finally able to maintain a fairly regular household routine. Since these were the ancient days before videos and DVDs, my only hope for long-term, sit-down kids' entertainment was *Sesame Street*. While my kids were mesmerized each weekday morning by Big Bird and Snuffleupagus, I had one hour of mommy time. During that one-hour time slot, I allotted 15 to 20 minutes for my time with God. I read a short passage from the Bible and poured out my heart to Him through intimate prayers. The more I practiced this discipline, the more I craved and cherished those minutes.

One particular morning, however, I was especially busy and stressed because some women from church were coming over for a meeting. Not only did I need to make the beds and plug in the coffeepot, I also wanted to tidy the clutter, wipe away fingerprints, and vacuum Cheerios from every nook and cranny in my home. As my kids were watching their morning show, I immersed myself in housekeeping chores and glanced at the clock now and then to see how much time I had left before my guests would arrive.

Isn't this the time you usually spend with Me? I heard someone say—not out loud, but somewhere in my head.

"But, God," I replied in defense, "these are my friends from *church,* and I'm practicing hospitality, which isn't even my spiritual gift. Doesn't that count?"

It was no use. I knew I would have no peace of mind unless I stopped for a few moments to spend some time in God's Word. I reached for my Bible and slipped my index finger between the pages that were already separated by my "World's Greatest Mom" book-mark—a recent Mother's Day gift from my cherubs. I began reading at the place where I had stopped the day before.

The passage I happened to read that morning was from Luke 10:38-42, which tells the story of Jesus at the home of His good friends, Mary and Martha. Martha was busy in the kitchen preparing food (and probably sweeping the floor) while Mary sat at the feet of Jesus, absorbing His every word. Martha was not pleased with her sister's lack of help.

"Lord, don't you care that my sister has left me to do the work by myself?" Martha asks Jesus. "Tell her to help me!"

Jesus' reply was not quite what Martha wanted to hear.

"Martha, Martha," the Lord answered, "you are worried and upset about many things, but only one thing is needed. Mary has chosen what is better."

Ouch! I may as well have read the verse using my name instead of Martha's, because I knew God was talking directly to me. I don't believe that God frowns on our cooking and cleaning, but I believe

He wants us to have balance in our lives and save time for some one-on-one with the One who knows us best. Each time we open the Bible and read its contents, we have the opportunity to sit at the feet of Jesus and absorb His words. When we talk to God in prayer, we can give our cares and concerns to our heavenly Father—the One who can manage it all better than we can. Spending time with God is cleansing and uplifting. It is encouraging and empowering. It is refreshing and energizing. And as busy moms, we can use all the help we can get.

When the doorbell rang, my house wasn't quite as clean as I had hoped it would be, but it was clean enough. The aroma of "almost ready" coffee permeated the air as we gathered around the kitchen table to have our meeting.

"Before we begin," I announced, "I'm going to read a short passage from Luke 10. It's something I recently read, and I'd like to share it with you."

After I read the Bible verses, I told my friends about my morning experience and how God reminded me that in the midst of my busyness, I needed to take time to be like Mary. Each woman agreed that we easily get caught up in our daily activities, and we need to make a conscious effort to spend some quality time with God.

As I poured the coffee and we began our meeting, I heard voices again—not in my head—they were loud and clear, and they were coming from our downstairs family room.

"Mom! *Sesame Street* is over."

rystal Bowman is a poet, speaker, lyricist, and author of more than 50 books for children and 3 books for women. Many of her story ideas come from the 25 years she spent raising her three children. She and her husband, Bob, have celebrated 34 years of marriage.

43

Goal Oriented

by Amy Bock

From the moment my son, Derek, was born, I'd thought about the day he'd be ready to play sports. My husband loves sports, and I knew when the ultrasound showed that we were having a little boy there was no denying the fact we'd be cheering him on for something. Secretly, I had always wanted to be a soccer mom. I wanted to be that parent with bumper stickers on the back of the minivan proclaiming to the world how proud I was of my athlete.

So the spring that Derek was old enough to join the local YMCA soccer league, we signed him up. My husband took him to get all the "proper" attire. We had to have the soccer shorts, the cleats, and the shin guards.

Derek practiced in the backyard every day getting ready for his first game. He was so excited! On the way out to the field he told us he was going to make 100 goals! He had all the confidence in the world. No doubt he was going to be a star player. In my mind he'd be ready for the Olympics in no time.

I practiced my cheers.

"Go, Derek!"

"Great goal!"

"Nice pass!"

We all arrived at the field and set up our chairs at the best viewing point. For the first 30 minutes of the session the kids practiced drills and worked with the coach. Then the moment came. It was game time. It was three on three with no goalie. It was…hilarious! I was not yelling all those things I'd practiced. Instead, it was more like, "Derek, your goal is the other one!"

"Not that way! Turn around!"

"Good try!"

Derek made two goals that day. He was so disappointed he cried all the way home. We tried to assure him that we were proud of him no matter how many goals he'd made and that he did a great job, but he would hear none of it. He, in his little four-year-old mind, had fallen way too short of his 100 goals.

Later that evening as I was thinking about the game, the goals, and the disappointment on the part of my son, I decided I was not any different. Derek practiced every day, but he was all by himself in our big backyard. When it came to game time, there were two different goals with five other children. He could easily make 100 goals at home, but with all the distractions on the field he was only able to make two.

When I became a mom, I can say I was confident in my abilities to be a mom. I had read the books, taken the classes, and had lofty goals. But then, somewhere between the sleep deprivation, colic, and changing hundreds of diapers I also became discouraged. Through this journey of mothering I have become distracted often and have been disappointed in myself more than once. Just as Derek had a hard time remembering which goal was his, I also forget the true goal of motherhood and feel as though I'm running in the wrong direction. But just as Derek had his mom and dad yelling directions from the sidelines, I have a heavenly Father gently guiding me through the chaos. In those rare quiet moments I can hear His voice.

"Good job, Amy."

"Nice mothering."

"Don't worry. Tomorrow is another day."

"I'm right here."

By listening closely to my Father, I can again find my direction and am able to keep my eyes on the goal. And I can imagine God cheering all of us moms on to victory. He's on our side. What a relief to know we have a voice of reason, a voice of encouragement, and a voice of sanity in those moments of motherhood that get us discouraged and disappointed. In the end I would like to be like Paul when he says in 2 Timothy 4:7-8 (NLT), "I have finished the race...and now the prize awaits me." That's the true goal of motherhood. Doing our best to help our kids love God, trust in Him, and finish the race that's before us.

Now that Derek is a couple years older I can say that I have shouted all those things I had practiced. He has become a much better soccer player, and I have become a much better soccer mom. The growing and learning never stops. The only constant is a loving parent on the sidelines with bumper stickers on the minivan.

*A*my Bock is a stay-at-home mom who lives in Lincoln, Nebraska, with her husband, Nick, and their two adorable children Derek (six) and Kylie (four). When she's not building LEGO castles or having My Little Pony tea parties, Amy enjoy cooking, reading, and writing.

44

The Face Before You

by Andrea Van Ye

Recently, I took my little girls ice-skating. Accompanying us was a very good friend of ours, Mrs. Strauss. She had cared for some of our younger children when one of our older children had undergone surgery on his legs. The Lord had provided Mrs. Strauss to our family during a very fragile and vulnerable time. She radiated love and care for all of us, and we were (ARE!) very fond of her. This time, however, she was not helping out, but rather along for the fun. She had decided not to skate, but she wanted to watch the children and encourage them in their "abilities."

We were at an indoor skating rink, and my five-year-old daughter, Lily Anne, well padded in her purple snow pants and jacket, with mittens and hat, made her way out to the middle of the ice rink. This was only the second time that Lily Anne had ever skated, so she was quite wobbly on her skates, her little ankles bending in and out with every attempt at a glide. But she was so excited about her newfound skills, and that her special friend, Mrs. Strauss, was there to see her.

After making the somewhat laborious journey from the edge of the rink out toward the middle, Lily Anne guardedly turned around. She then spotted Mrs. Strauss, who was standing up on a ramp, separated from her by a large Plexiglas wall. The rink was also used for hockey games. The Plexiglas was marked up with scratches and smudges, looking rather distorted and dirty, but Mrs. Strauss could still be seen through the thin, opaque barrier.

Lily Anne was moving her feet ever so carefully and gingerly, arms outstretched, with her face shining upward toward Mrs. Strauss. Shuffle. Glide. Pause. Shuffle. Glide. Pause. She was concentrating, trying to maintain an upright posture, with legs and feet in reasonable distance and stance. A smile radiated from her face. Occasionally, she would wobble. Sometimes, she would almost lose her balance. Intermittently, she would fall. SPLAT! KERPLUNK! Like a baby horse learning how to walk shortly after being born, Lily Anne's legs would go out from underneath her, and then she would wiggle and waggle to get up again. No matter what, her eyes would rarely look away from Mrs. Strauss.

When I followed Lily Anne's eyes to Mrs. Strauss, I was taken aback by what I saw. There our dear friend stood, on the other side of that Plexiglas wall. She was smiling and cheering. She clapped her hands, and her eyes and face said, "Good job, Lily Anne! You can do it!" We could not hear her, but we did not need to. Her beautiful, enthusiastic, loving, radiant face said it all. It did not matter whether Lily Anne tripped, wobbled, or even fell. Mrs. Strauss just kept on cheering her on. She never looked disappointed. She did not walk away because Lily Anne was not perfect at what she was doing. She loved Lily Anne, and Lily Anne knew it. All Lily Anne had to do was see Mrs. Strauss's face. That's all it took. She kept on getting up and getting her bearings. Trying. Focusing. Persevering. Eager to get to Mrs. Strauss with no condemnation or fear.

I stood there in the middle of the ice that day, and tears filled my eyes. I thought, *Why can't I remember that that is how God looks at me?* He is standing there, on the other side of the thin shield that separates me from Him; He is right there. He sees what I am doing. He is standing there, smiling at me. Cheering me on. He is focused on me. He is not disappointed when I stumble, or wobble, or fall.

He is there, waiting for me, arms outstretched, loving me. I need to remember that when I am struggling as a mom or as a woman. (And even when I am not struggling.) He stands ready for us. He says to us "I love you. I delight in you. You are Mine. There is no condemnation. You do not need to be afraid. I have my eyes on you. Keep trying. I will never leave you."

Andrea Van Ye resides in Neenah, Wisconsin, with her husband and five children. She enjoys reading, writing, running, and teaching Bible study. Her passion as a mother and a woman is to encourage her children, as well as other women, to seek God and embrace His unfailing love for them.

Siblings, Side by Side

45

Brotherly Love

by Susie Larson

How did the retreat go?" I was hoping for a good report since this weekend was Luke's initiation into the youth group.

Jake got in the car, scooted right next to the door, and leaned his head against the window. Luke unassumingly hopped in behind him, not picking up on the hint that Jake wanted his space.

Luke struggled with ADD. He was sick a lot as a child and had regular problems with asthma. He was strong willed, a bit awkward socially, and things didn't come as easy for him as they did for Jake.

"Did you make any new friends, Luke?" Luke, who tended to make mountains out of molehills (and vice versa), casually said, "It went okay. I almost died three times, but otherwise it was fun."

I looked back over the seat and asked, "*What* did you say?"

In a matter-of-fact way, Luke proceeded to tell me that though his chest was tight from an asthma flare up, Jake's friends held him under water until he was gasping for air. They called him names, ditched him, teased him, and shoved him around.

The more the story unfolded, the more I felt compelled to bring back the Lamaze breathing techniques I used when he was born. Focus and breathe. Focus and breathe. Not a bad idea for parents with adolescent boys.

I had a question for my other son.

"Where were *you* when all this was happening, Jake?" He answered, "Huh? Well, I was around. Luke was bugging us."

Being absolutely furious with my son, I realized I needed to take a breather before I could address what happened. I turned up the song on the radio, and we had a quiet ride home. I needed wisdom for this situation.

When I talked with other mothers about the sibling issue, their responses were always the same. "Boys will be boys," "Get used to it; it's normal," or "There's not much you can do about it."

And yet every time I went to Scripture I could find nothing to support such an idea. Nowhere did it say that cold love was something to get used to or accept as normal. On the contrary; God's call was a high one: "By this all men will know that you are my disciples, if you love one another" (John 13:35).

I felt an inner restraint compelling me to wait for the right time to talk with Jake. For three days I prayed fervently that God would prepare his heart and mine too. Finally the day came, and I knew it was time.

I started out, "Jake, I want you to know that your dad and I love you so very much. We love how you love Jesus. We love that you're involved at church and that you have lots of friends. We love that you do well in school and that you're so respectful to us as your parents."

Jake cracked a smile. I continued. "But I would trade all of these things if you would just love your brother. In fact, I would go so far as to say that your Christianity is only as valid as your love is for the most irritating person in your life. And right now, that person is Luke.

"The fact that you could be so selfish while your own brother was being treated so poorly tells me that your heart is further away than your actions reveal. And though you look real good on the outside, you're standing only an inch tall, spiritually speaking. I am deeply troubled by your cold heart and I think you should be too."

Jake just stared at me. I went on. "I want you to remember that Luke has as much right to be here as you do. He is a part of this family, and we love him as much as we love you. He's a part of me, Jake, and when you look at him with eyes of contempt, you're looking at me that way."

Quietly Jake replied, "You're right, Mom. You're right."

"Honey, I know what I'm asking of you is going to cost you something. You are going to have to dig deep to love Luke when he's not acting very lovable. I'm asking you to take the higher road. I'm asking you to make allowances for his faults. Often boys your age think it's cool to act like they're too cool for their families, but the true sign of maturity is when someone is kind to his family and too secure to care what others think. That's what I want for you, Jake.

"There's one more thing, son. Since it was you who paved the way for your friends to treat Luke this way, I want you to be part of the solution. Luke needs a fresh new youth group experience. For the next two weeks I want you to take Luke to a large youth gathering a few miles from here. I want this for two reasons: One, because you owe it to him. And two, because I respect your opinion and want to know if you think this is a good place for him."

Jake's only words were, "Okay, Mom. I will do it."

The night came and I drove the boys to the youth meeting. I sat out in the foyer and watched on the television screen as kids worshiped and listened to a powerful message.

The doors opened up and hundreds of teens streamed out of the doors and flooded the lobby. I stood on my toes trying to catch a glimpse of my boys. Luke wasn't in my view, but I could see Jake shuffling my way. His eyes were to the ground and he looked sad.

I reached him, put my hands on his shoulders, and said, "What, honey? What's wrong?" With tear-filled eyes he looked up at me and said, "Oh, Mom. I've been so wrong! God showed me I've been keeping an account against my own brother. Even when he wasn't wrong, I treated him as though he was. I got down on my knees, surrendered my list, and asked God for forgiveness. Now I have to ask you. Will you forgive me for how I've treated your son?"

Completely overwhelmed, I wrapped my arms around Jake and we cried together, surrounded by a sea of teenagers.

From that point on, Jake made a conscious effort to be good to his brother. Jake invited him places, he laughed at his goofy jokes, and he began to really love Luke.

Over the years, a miracle happened before our very eyes. The awkward adolescence in Luke disappeared and no traces remain. Luke has grown into a humble, solid, godly young man. He is studying to be a worship pastor, and he and Jake are the best of friends.

Of all the work we put into Luke, it was the love of his brother that transformed his life. The impact of a sibling's love is life changing. I understand now more than ever why it's important that we love one another.

I owe Jake a debt of gratitude for digging deep and going the extra mile when it wasn't natural or instinctive to do so. His willingness to love changed our family, and I will always be grateful to him.

Susie Larson is an author, speaker, and a freelance writer for *Focus on the Family*. Susie has been married to Kevin (the love of her life) since 1985, and they have three almost-grown sons: Jake (22), Luke (20), and Jordan (18). Susie says that the most rewarding thing about being a mom is watching her sons be such great friends, and watching them all follow Jesus. For more information, visit her website at www.susielarson.com.

46

We Can Both Dance

by Julia Pryor

As a toddler, our youngest daughter, Jane, showed patience beyond her years. She was a good sport—she really enjoyed going with her family on the MANY trips that took place for church events, medical appointments, school activities, and sporting events.

This girl logged many miles in her car seat, yet she was somehow thrilled to accompany anyone on any type of trip to a store. Always well behaved, and with unbridled enthusiasm for all things retail, she would coo with delight if we even passed a shopping area. Her first actual sentence was "go yopping"—meaning "go shopping."

This could not have been a more ironic twist. As parents, we shopped only when absolutely necessary. This fascination of hers appeared inborn.

Our family was ALWAYS on a budget—A TIGHT budget. We were always looking for the bargains and purchased only what was needed. Trips to shopping malls were planned in advance and not spontaneous affairs. We made the most out of every trip, and overall this was a positive, if infrequent, experience for the family.

Shoe shopping was somewhat of a major event, and our budget was to buy one new pair of shoes each month (with a few exceptions). We

175

started with the kid that needed shoes the most and rotated around the family. Youngest daughter Jane, the "go yopping" one, had gone along on many of these shopping trips.

For months she watched as the others were fitted with their new pair. During each visit to the shoe store, she spotted her favorite pair on the display rack. She had selected her pair of shoes months before it was her turn to actually buy them.

They were pastel pink-and-white saddle shoes—no Velcro, no buckles, but good old-fashioned pastel pink-and-white leather tie shoes. Time passed, and each month she would enter the store and select the same shoes. She would cradle these shoes in her arms, but she knew she would have to wait her turn. She was amazingly patient.

Finally it was Jane's turn, and she was anticipating the day. The entire family could see the glow of happy excitement she carried with her.

Once at the store, she made a beeline to the shoes, *her* shoes, the ones she had been waiting for. She was a toddler on a mission! This was the fastest day of shoe shopping on record. The shoes were finally purchased. Jane jumped for joy and walked out of the store with her shoes on. She leaped, she hopped, she skipped, and she danced in her shoes. She even slept in her shoes, and it was precious. She loved those shoes and cared for them unlike any other toddler that I have ever seen.

A few weeks later, our oldest boy, James, was having a birthday. The day before his birthday a tornado hit Grandma's house, and Dad headed down to help with the cleanup. This birthday dinner was a defining moment, a rite of passage: James turned double digits, but Dad was not at the table. The birthday boy assumed the head position at the table. This position, while once anticipated with glee, was suddenly not as good as he thought it would be. The room was somehow off balance.

The atmosphere at dinner was unusually serious as we listened to the storms overhead. My attempts at lightening the mood were met with an unfamiliar silence as all our thoughts went to Grandma and Dad. It was turning into the kind of day you just wanted to get through and forget about.

All of a sudden little Jane held up a finger indicating she would be right back. Without saying a word, she ran to another room. Moments later she returned to the table acting like a royal princess carrying a crown disguised as a living room pillow. On the pillow she had a gift, hastily wrapped in a bath towel.

With a shining smile on her face, she announced to the birthday boy, "It's for you."

Confused, James asked, "What is it?"

"It's a present to make you happy," Jane replied. "Open it."

James took the pillow, and opened the gift. He saw one shoe, one pink-and-white saddle shoe. Toddler girl-sized given to this robust sixth-grade boy.

Jane was smiling, standing happily ostrichlike on one foot. She absolutely beamed at her brother. Around the table were the muffled laughs of the rest of the kids, all with confused looks on their faces.

James said, "Thanks, Jane." And then he asked the obvious question, "Why are you giving me your shoe, ONE shoe?"

We all listened as Jane answered, not skipping a beat. "Now we can both be happy, and we can both dance!"

Then she hopped happily out of the room.

She had given her brother something that meant the world to her. Even if it meant she was left with one shoe. She could still dance, and in her eyes so could he. It turned out to be a birthday we will always remember.

*J*ulia Hill Pryor and husband, Daniel, are blessed with seven children and wouldn't trade a moment. Jennifer (Dave) Crutchfield, James (MacKenzie), Joseph, John, Jaclyn, Jane, and Jeffrey: joys, all! Julia is active in church, sports, and school activities. She works for University of Illinois Extension.

47

More Than I Bargained For

by Kelly Hughes

It was sonogram day. It wasn't something that was new to me, the whole sonogram experience. I had a beautiful two-year-old son. We had sonograms before, so this was routine. I was a mom already, and frankly, I had it all under control. This growing boy that my husband and I were raising was relatively easy. I really wasn't sure what all the fuss and bother about parenting was—it seemed pretty fun. Adding one more baby to the family was going to be great. It would come with challenges, I knew, but it would be great. I was organized. I was in control.

So on sonogram day, my husband and I went in looking forward to the nearly undistinguishable snapshot of our baby. You know, the ones that only the parents seem to be able to see their child in. We were 20 weeks along at that time. The technician got out the cold gel and grabbed her wand. As she began to scan my tummy and look at the picture on the screen, she casually asked, "Have you felt a little big?"

Felt a little big? What kind of question is that for an expectant mom? I had felt a little big since the birth of my first child! I thought that was just another part of being a mom. I do admit, though, that I had been sneaking around wearing maternity clothes for a few weeks now—the rubber band on the button of my jeans and such—not wanting to admit I was already showing...or perhaps it was just all the chocolate I had been snitching? Anyway, don't you show more quickly with your second pregnancy?

"A little," I said, "but my dates are right...my husband was out of town in the fall."

"Oh, your dates are right," she said. "It's just that there are two babies."

Two babies? Two babies? Twins? This was not part of the plan. One new baby I could handle, but two? My husband and I had continued the playful argument since we got married...he wanted two kids, I wanted three. But that third baby was supposed to come in another two and a half years. The plan, you know!

"Well, you always get your way," was David's soft response (with that "can you believe this is happening" grin). The technician printed off the picture for us. Sure enough, there it was in fuzzy black-and-white—two heads, four hands, twenty tiny fingers, and twenty little toes.

The technician probably said several very sweet and encouraging things to my husband and me as she continued the scan. Not that we really heard all that much. She asked us if we wanted to know what the sex of each of the babies was. I was ready to know (I need to make plans), but David wasn't quite ready for the additional information. He needed a little time.

It took us about six hours to regain some sort of normal brain function and become verbal again. We ended up calling the hospital back that afternoon to find out we were expecting two girls—and from the looks of things, identical girls. We were overwhelmed at what stood before us. Thousands of questions entered my mind, from the practical to the outrageous. We only have one crib...hey, we only have one of EVERYTHING! Our house is too small. How will we afford it? Two weddings? Do we dress them alike? What happened to my control?

That evening we called my parents to tell them the news. My dad, after sitting quietly for a moment, told me with firm resolve that whatever challenges were ahead with these new babies, we would face it all together. Wow. I had started this day thinking that I was in control and life was predictable. By the end of the day, I learned yet again that God is in control. I learned that God's plans are the best plans—even when they aren't mine—and contain so much more joy than I could ever imagine in my own limited thinking. I learned that God has put people in our lives so we don't have to face challenges alone. That special day we got more than we bargained for. More blessings than this mom could have ever have imagined.

Kelly Hughes lives in Bloomington, Illinois, with her husband, David, and their children: Jeremiah, Nichole, and Jennifer. She is the Senior Director of Conference Production with Hearts at Home. In her spare time, you can find her hanging out with her family (especially at Disney World) or reading something about the Civil War.

48

Just Like...

by Jennifer Noble

Looking at my three children, I note that their personalities reflect who they are but also shed light for me as a mom. I am the mother of two daughters and one son—in that order. From my parents I am the firstborn daughter with one younger brother. Oftentimes I look at my oldest daughter, Lana, and I see myself. Our birth order matches, and there are many things we have in common. She bosses her younger sister around just the way I used to do. She organizes her brother and sister for the next game or play activity. She is a chip off the old block.

Then there's my youngest daughter, Sierra—frequently making me wonder where my DNA is represented. She reminds me of my brother, only she's a little sister. Full of adventure and peacemaking at the same time, I try to figure her out. I wonder which relative she is most like. She has some of the characteristics of her uncle and her grandpa, and a few of the antics of our humorous great-aunt all mixed together. She's always surprising me.

I saw a stark contrast between us when we would have her well-baby checkups through her first year. I am a woman who dreads doctor appointments. I despise needles. If I can get through the checkup without any blood work, I'm celebrating. Sierra made it through every appointment without a single tear. This was amazing to me. *She's my daughter?* I thought to myself. I go to help her and end up feeling virtually useless. A quick signing of the paperwork, and I turn my head for the shots. But Sierra manages her vaccinations with barely a flinch. After her appointments, we'd make a routine phone call to Grandma. She would ask about the visit, and I would remark, "Sierra didn't cry again. Can you believe it?" I was awed time after time.

As the girls continued to get older, I wondered how they would get along. I hoped they would share the close bond I enjoyed with my brother growing up. I hoped they wouldn't waste their precious time together with issues of jealousy or sibling rivalry, and they were doing well for the most part. It seemed very comparable to the dynamics I had experienced. But I soon began to see how closely I needed to watch myself.

It was the month of Lana's kindergarten physical. She began worrying and fretting about it after hearing reports from preschool classmates. Lana started with questions about the shots, wondering if they would hurt. I told her there would only be a little pinch, but inside my stomach was curdling.

I remembered those kindergarten shots. After that experience, nurses couldn't handle me and my parents dreaded every fever and annual sports physical. I soon had to lie down for even a little finger prick. And it wasn't limited to the doctor. My dentist referred me on to someone else after I passed out in his chair. This had been an embarrassment—and I didn't want Lana's experiences to mirror mine.

To make the kindergarten shots easier on us, I told Lana we would schedule her appointment with her brother's monthly baby checkup. It would be smoother, I had hoped, with them both going in on the same day. Week after week we reviewed the plan. "You will get your shots the same day as your brother. It's in three weeks." "Two weeks." "Grandma asked us to call as soon as we are done." She was anxious and prayerful right along with us. I kept trying to anticipate what was coming. One week left. And then it was here!

I called in the troops and Daddy came from work. The nurses were smart, deciding Lana should go before her brother. They told her to count to ten through the injection. Everyone in the whole doctor's office could hear our numeration through the walls. And then it was over. We had made it! There were sticker books, suckers, and flashy stickers. I thought I should qualify for the prizes too. We were beaming. On the way home, we kept reminding Lana of how she was set for kindergarten. She had done so well and was ready for her "big girl" class.

We immediately called Grandma to tell her all about the experience. As Lana began the conversation with Grandma, something shook me. The first words out of my daughter's mouth were totally unexpected. Lana was proud of a moment, which for us had gone unrealized. "Grandma, I got my shots today. And I didn't even cry."

The next phrase is what blew me away. "Just like Sierra."

All those times she had heard me admire Sierra for not crying at her doctor's appointments had made an impact on her. I realized how much my approval meant—the excitement in my voice or the surprises I have. Even though my children will experience similar things, it's their experience, and they want their mom to take note. I need to be careful in how I praise them and think about what may cross their minds. Lana's experience brought about a change in me that day. After she hung up the phone, I gave her one more hug. "I'm so proud of *you*."

Jennifer Noble lives in South Dakota where she is mom to three and writes for numerous publications. Her blog is www.easyreadingpicks.blogspot.com. Jennifer is involved in marriage ministries with her husband, Chad, Hearts at Home, and MOPS, and she enjoys prayer times through Moms in Touch and serving Billy Graham's Rapid Response team.

Learn from the Best

49

Partner in Prayer

by Pam Farrel

We believe in keeping track of prayer requests. Prayer is simply talking to God about your kids, right? Sometimes we might wonder if God is listening. Let me share one prayer request I made for my son, Brock, when he was a baby.

> *God, give Brock the courage to stand alone for You. Give him the integrity and wisdom to choose well in his relationships and lead him to the godly woman he will marry someday.*

Does God answer when we partner with Him in prayer? You be the judge.

We were at the first football game in which Brock was to be the starting varsity quarterback. He was only a junior, but God had already used him to bring many of his friends to faith in Christ, and Brock had started a Fellowship of Christian Athletes (FCA) club on his campus.

As a freshman, Brock wanted to make a positive difference, so we encouraged him to host three pizza parties for the three teams he was on, and at those parties Brock shared his personal testimony and the gospel and gave his friends an opportunity to meet Christ. By the end of his freshman year, 34 of his friends had made decisions for Christ. Realizing they needed to be followed up with so they could grow with God, Brock contacted FCA and launched a club on the campus his sophomore year.

Brock wanted to make a public statement for his faith, so he called up his buddies on the team and said, "This week, after we beat Fallbrook, I'm going to the 50 yard line to pray. Will you join me?" They all said, "We're there for ya, man!"

Bill and I prayed for and with Brock that morning, and then my Moms in Touch prayer group joined in later. That night Brock's team lost 38-0. The guys just wandered off the field—all except Brock, who went straight to the 50 yard line and knelt down—all alone.

Standing near my husband, I said to Bill, "Honey, he's all alone! Should I run down and pray with him?" My wise husband said, "Oh yeah, Pam. That's what the varsity quarterback wants—his mommy to come rescue him!"

Just then I remembered the prayer we had prayed years ago. *Help him stand alone for You, God.* And now he was. God answers prayer.

Soon, three players from the opposing team joined Brock and they prayed. After the game some of Brock's youth leaders from Student Venture and Fellowship of Christian Athletes went down to encourage Brock. Then we made our way to the field.

I threw my arms around my son. Reaching up, I took his face in my hands and said, "I have never been more proud of you than I am at this moment. I know tonight was one of the hardest nights of your life—but you kept your word to God. Remember what we always tell you, 'Those who honor God, God honors.' Brock, I don't know how and I don't know when, but God will honor you for this."

God has continued to be true to his promise in Psalm 84:11, "No good thing does he withhold from those whose walk is blameless." During Brock's senior year he was named Athlete of the Year, he was named to the National Hall of Fame for Football for a Scholar Leader, and he was named San Diego Citizen of the Year (and that came with a commendation from the governor and a scholarship from the NFL

Retired Player's Association). He was also given our high school's highest award for servant leadership, Knight of the Year. The faculty votes on it, and when they gave him the award, they stood and gave him a standing ovation. God answers prayer.

Brock went on to attend a junior college that he selected because the coach was a committed believer, active in FCA, and a man who mentored his players. Brock helped teach a Bible study for 18 months while attending a class that helped him learn how to defend his faith. He caught the heart for helping people find answers to their spiritual questions. God answers prayer.

Brock was named MVP, Mission Conference Player of the Year, and awarded All State-Player honors. God answers prayer.

We had sent Brock's profile to all the Division 1 and Division 1AA schools. Being a 6' quarterback meant he needed a miracle to get a scholarship despite his record-breaking throwing record. In addition, Bill had experienced some health issues and was in a career transition, so we also needed that miracle scholarship. One night God woke me up with the impression: "Send Brock's résumé to Liberty University tonight." The next day the coach from Liberty phoned Brock's coach. We had never seen him so excited as when he signed that Letter of Intent. God answers prayer.

Since Brock's birth, we have prayed for his future bride. When Brock had been at Liberty just a few days, I spoke in Phoenix and did a book signing for Amazing Grace Christian Bookstore. While there, I struck up a conversation with the bookstore owner and his wife. Sheryl asked me, "Where did you say Brock got his scholarship?"

"He's the quarterback of Liberty University."

"My Hannah goes to Liberty!"

We gave the kids each other's phone numbers and our two strong-willed firstborn kids decided to go on a date! After 18 months of dating and after they spent a week in prayer, Brock took Hannah on a tour of their relationship. They had not even kissed yet to safeguard their purity. At the place they first met he gave her nails, at the place they first talked seriously, he gave her a hammer, at the place they first prayed, he gave her a piece of wood, and at the home she was living in with friends, he gave her a second piece of wood which they hammered together to form a cross. He knelt on one knee next to the cross and said, "I want our relationship to start at the foot of the cross. Hannah, will you marry me? Hannah, can I kiss you?"

On July 25, 2005, Brock and Hannah tied the knot and became husband and wife. God answers prayer. Today Brock is a football coach, equipping young men, and Hannah is expecting their first child—so the prayers for our grandchild have begun!

*P*am Farrel is mom to three and wife to Bill. Together they have penned more than 27 books, including *10 Best Decisions a Parent Can Make*. Pam also coauthored *Got Teens?* with Hearts at Home founder Jill Savage. Pam offers many free relationship resources for marriage and family at www.farrelcommunications.com.

50

Cool Mom

by Karen Brundieck

The day began much like any other. I was busy with all the jobs a mother of four children can find herself buried under. My children were trying to find some way to keep themselves occupied on an early summer day. It seemed like an ordinary day.

After wandering around trying to find something to do, my children and a neighbor child or two came running into the kitchen. My daughter clutched in her sweaty hand a packet of sunflower seeds that she had gotten a few weeks earlier in Sunday school.

"Mom! Can we plant these seeds?" They all eagerly crowded around me with upturned faces brimming with excitement. I was busy making dinner and didn't want to bother with figuring out the logistics of where and how they would plant the seeds. The no that came all too readily to my lips almost slipped out. I was tired and busy and didn't want to mess with it.

"Please, Mom?" My daughter's eyes implored even more urgently than her voice.

"I guess so," I replied, surprising even myself. I stifled a sigh and rinsed the flour off my hands. "I think I have some pots in the garage."

I took a few moments to locate some miniature pots that had been lying around on a shelf. I found a bag of potting soil, rounded up a trowel, and handed everything off to them.

"I have to finish dinner. Make sure you clean up when you are done."

A chorus of voices assured me they would, so I went back inside to finish my cooking. I must admit I enjoyed the quiet that enveloped the house while everyone was busy outside. In no time at all, I had dinner in the oven and had cleaned up my kitchen. I thought I would check to see if they had in fact cleaned up the garage, so I stuck my head out the door.

They were sitting in a circle on the cement floor in the garage, admiring their pots filled with dirt.

"Do you think they will grow?" I heard the neighbor girl ask my daughter.

"We have to water them," my daughter replied. "I'm going to put mine out on the back step so it will get wet when it rains."

"I can't believe your mom let us plant these. You have such a cool mom."

"Yeah, I know."

I eased back into the kitchen and shut the door. A cool mom? Me? And all because I let them plant a few seeds? If I had ever thought I would arrive in the ranks of "cooldom," I would never have guessed that it would be in such a simple way. I was sure that such status was reserved for mothers who fearlessly hosted 12 giggling girls for a sleepover or willingly served as den leader for Cub Scouts. Or surely it would require something as noteworthy as being brave enough to Rollerblade with the children, or even dive off the high diving board. Isn't that what makes a cool mother?

As I stood there thinking about it, I realized that I had grossly underestimated the power of saying yes. It had been such a small thing. I gave them some pots, some dirt, and left them alone. But to them it had been something big. It was something they wanted to do, and instead of brushing it off with an impatient no, I had said yes. With a sinking heart, I realized I didn't do that very often. It was usually easier, less messy, and less time-consuming to say no to some of the things my children took in their heads to do.

My thoughts were interrupted when the children burst into the house to show me their pots full of dirt. I admired them and assured the neighbor children they could take theirs home. I praised the job they had done of sweeping up all the dirt in the garage.

Time went on. No flowers grew, and the pots sat forlorn on the back step. My children became busy with the activities of summer and forgot all about the seeds they had planted, but I did not. The lesson I learned that day continued to influence me. Whenever my children would come to me for permission to do anything, the memory of those pots would check the no that rose automatically to my lips. I would listen, really listen, to what they were asking to do, and if it was possible to give permission, I would do so. It did mean that there were more messes around than I liked to see, and sometimes I would have to endure a noise level above what I was comfortable with. But I realized that little things mean a lot to a child. By moving out of my comfort zone a bit, I could easily accommodate those requests. Just watching the faces of my children light up when they were told they could build tents in the living room, or get out the bead sets with a gazillion pieces and make some jewelry, assured me that I had learned my lesson from the day I was a cool mom.

*K*aren has been married 20 years to her best friend, Mark. She homeschools her four children: Matthew (17), Melissa (12), Lydia (10), and Adam (8). She enjoys reading, writing, history, and taking on new challenges such as learning to ice-skate, knit, and play the piano.

51

A Birthday Surprise

by Christie Todd

It was a cold February day. My son, Nathan, was having his ninth birthday party, and he received a new skateboard as one of his gifts. He was dying to try it out, so I told him he could ride it a few times in the house but he had to be careful.

Things seemed to be going well at first. But it wasn't long until I heard the loud sounds of him crashing into objects of my household, each time saying, "Don't worry, Mom. I'm all right!" To be truthful, it wasn't him I was worried about, but everything else in the house. Wondering if I was insane for allowing him to ride inside in the first place, I yelled from the other room, "It's time to stop and put the skateboard away. You can use it outside when it gets warmer." I wanted him to have fun since it was his birthday, but I had had enough of the skateboard in the house.

I moved on, trying to complete the task at hand, when I heard an even louder sound, a crash that sounded as though it could have done some damage. Having a day care in my home, loud noises are common, so I took a deep breath and hoped for the best. I overheard my daughter gasp, and then she ran by laughing, with her hand over her mouth.

"What happened?" I asked. I heard no response except for my daughter's taunting to her brother about getting in trouble. Soon after, he slowly entered the room with his head down.

"Mom, I have something to tell you," he said.

"What happened, Nathan?"

"Why don't we go in my room and sit down," was his reply. I knew it must be bad. As we sat in his room, through tears he explained to me how when I asked him to put the skateboard away, he wasn't quite ready. He wanted to try just one more trick, and the trick ended badly with the skateboard hitting the wall in our family room. He explained that the result was a dent in the wall. I immediately left his room to evaluate the situation.

I gasped and covered my mouth when I saw that there was not just an indentation, but the skateboard had broken through the drywall and left a large gaping hole. His words and tears told me how sorry he was, and I appreciated and accepted his apology, but sorry alone was not going to cut it this time. In our house you are expected to obey, and because he had not obeyed me, there were consequences for him to pay. Consequences that would help him remember not to make the same mistake the next time he was in a similar situation.

Later, I considered this lesson in my own life. There have been times when I have said, "Just one more time" when I know God has clearly asked me to stop. I don't always remember the consequences of the last bad decision I made in life. I can easily forget the lessons learned in the past.

Yet God continues to show me grace and remind me that I am not self-sufficient and that I need Him for everything. I need to obey Him in the same way I expect my children to obey me. This is just one of the many lessons God has taught me through my children. When I am frustrated by the disobedient actions of my son or daughter, I have to stop and remind myself that I have done the same thing to my heavenly Father. I am His child, and He calls me to obey Him. And when I do, hopefully, my children will learn a lesson in obedience from me.

Christie Todd resides in Chenoa, Illinois, with her husband of 13 years, Mike, and their two wonderful children, Elizabeth (12) and Nathan (10). Her passion is to tell others about what God has done in her life. She is an inspirational speaker with Awaken the Heart Ministries (www.awakentheheartministries.com).

52

Grandmother at 37

by Jan Kwasigroh

Grandmother"—Webster defines a grandmother as the mother of one's father or mother; or a term of respectful familiarity to any elderly woman. If that were all there was to being a grandmother, life would be oh so dull. The ache or emptiness that I felt when our three adult children left for college/marriage/jobs was not appeased until our first grandchild was born.

Nobody told me what that instant would bring to me. Nobody told me it would happen over and over with each additional grandchild until I now feel as though I am bursting inside with unasked for love and pride. Also, nobody told me I would cheerfully lose at cards and marble games, and stock the refrigerator with chocolate milk, caffeine-free drinks, frozen pizzas, ice-cream bars, and even keep a snack drawer that, with permission, small hands can dive into before going home. Nobody told me that jokingly calling my three-year-old grandson, Chris, by the name of "Fred" would cause him to ask his mother for some paper and crayons to "make a name tag so the next time I go to Grandma's she'll remember my name."

I'd also forgotten that when I give little tips to my grandchildren these will undoubtedly get passed along to other children. "Spitting is not permitted" is the word I got during vacation Bible school, and I knew where it came from—my grandkids telling other kids how to behave using my very words.

Two-thirds of my grandkids live many miles away, so the chance to cuddle, talk, play with, and just be with them happens not nearly as often as I would like. By buying a book in their age and interest, recording the story with a "please turn the page" reminder, and then sending the book and tape to them, they could have some of Grandma whenever they wanted. It did throw their dad off a bit one time when, coming up the stairs, he heard my voice reading and wondered when I had arrived in town.

I don't feel older than when my three children were growing up, but I realized sometime ago that the years do add up. I decided early on that Jack Benny had used 39 as his perpetual age, so I chose 37. For years, and I mean years, I told anyone who asked that I was 37. Until one day when a grandson asked me how come his daddy "was older than you, Grandma?" Guess it was time to move along on the time line.

Becoming a grandmother also meant I would become a listening board, a tool I didn't use often as a mom. While I don't always have advice, nor do I offer it unless asked, I do see things from a different perspective now. I am no longer the frazzled mom, being bombarded from all sides for clean socks, lunch money, missing homework papers, signed permission slips gone AWOL, an almost empty gas tank, a missed school bus, or never-ending hunger pangs. The list is endless, but I now see these things as just minor glitches in the stream of life. If I can run the car pool or ease the frustration in my adult children's families in any way, I will—not only for the parents but for me—'cause then I get my grandkid fix!

I don't know how to pass to my grown children the fact that their time with their own children remains so precious and that the wonders of childhood are fleeting. After-school programs—whether they are sports, gymnastics, music, choir, or church-related education—tend to take all the kids' free time to just "be." No riding bicycles, impromptu neighborhood games, reading for pleasure, helping Mom in the kitchen or Dad in the yard/garage. Those things are just not there anymore. This drive to excel at everything leaves no time to fantasize, become best buddies, or just be a kid. While TV offers a fantastic array of programs and the computer games can teach just about anything, both are solitary activities.

Oh, you can take turns at computer games, but where does one learn the friendly frustration and good sportsmanship that happens when their marble gets sent back to start or the cards don't match as quickly as another player's do? Learning to press on, start over (and over and over in some cases), and eventually win is an ecstatic feeling.

And my grandkids don't let Grandma forget that SHE lost and THEY won. But that's okay, 'cause at age 37 I have lots of playing years still in me!

*J*an and her retired Air Force husband, Larry, have three wonderful children and are grandparents to ten fantastic youngsters. She is currently looking for ways to bottle the energy and love these kids have in abundance.

53

Listen with Your Eyes
by Bridget Nelan

The day was just like many others. By 7:00 a.m. I wished I'd set the alarm earlier. Although summer break was in full swing and there weren't any tardy bells to try and beat, the days were busy. In my attempt to maintain some order over the summer, I signed the kids up for some activities, allowing enough downtime and playtime to keep them from burning out. Yet each day was busy with juggling different activities, keeping the house in order, and getting dinner on the table. If I had my druthers, I'd just play all day with my children, but then chaos and clutter would take over.

The kids were full of energy that day. There were the usual schedules to meet, piles to get through (mail, papers, laundry, etc.), and mouths to feed. My children were relatively well behaved, with their fighting staying at a moderate level, one that I didn't fear impending injury. I was getting some chores done and no blood had been shed. Overall, I felt I was juggling my duties as a mom, balancing the daily demands, and (for the most part) keeping my voice down.

What I didn't know and wasn't prepared for that day when I woke was how one sentence out of my child's mouth was about to change my modus operandi. The day had flown by, as they all do, and it was time to start thinking about dinner. I remember the scene exactly. I was at the kitchen sink attempting to thaw out some meat that I should have thought about hours earlier. The natives were getting restless, and I was feeling squeezed for time and running low on patience. One of my children was at the table working on something. He said, "Hey, Mom, you know what?"

"What?" I replied. He began telling me something that seemed a bit trivial, but as I later learned, was not trivial to him.

"Are you listening, Mama?"

"Of course, honey. Keep talking. I'm listening." But was I really? I thought I was, just like my husband probably thinks he's listening to me recite the grocery list as he reads the newspaper. The next minute must have taken place in slow motion because it is imprinted in my memory. I felt a tug on my shirt.

When I turned around, my son was looking up at me, his big blue eyes dancing. I dried my hands and bent down. He took my face in his hands and said, "Mom. Listen to me with your eyes."

The gut check was a real one. *Listen to me with your eyes.* Wow. How long had my attention been so haphazard? Multitasking had been a way of life for me for as long as I can remember. Before marriage, before kids, postkids…I remember how I felt that day, at the kitchen sink, as I stopped what I was doing, emptied my mind, and focused on my child. I smiled and felt my heart smile. I silently thanked God for teaching me this lesson before my children were raised and gone. I don't remember if the meat got thawed or what exactly we had for dinner that night, but I'm certain we ate something. I do remember, though, how good it felt to stop, focus, and listen with my ears as well as my eyes.

I have to admit it is still a struggle for me to slow down, savor the precious moments of each day, and live, just live. But when I take the time to ask for guidance through prayer, the answers usually come when I listen with my eyes. My children, spouse, family, and friends all deserve the best I have to give, so each day I strive to do as my little boy asked me to do that day at the kitchen sink. I listen with my eyes. And someday when my little boy isn't so little anymore, I will teach him a great lesson that he taught me as a little boy…how to listen with his eyes.

Bridget Nelan is married to Mark with all boys, ages 4 through 20. Her passion is her family—experiencing new adventures, sports, and everyday life with them. She's also a writer and enjoys music and travel. She loves being a mom because her children make her feel God's presence each day.

Section Ten

Let Go with Love

54

Daddy's Travels

by Jill Briscoe

I've been asked to visit America," Stuart told me one day, as our three rambunctious children clattered around our tiny house.

"Ooooh," said David. "Where's that?"

"It's far away across the sea," Stuart told him. We lived in England, working and ministering at the Capernwray School. But Stuart had the heart of an evangelist and a gift for preaching, and requests for him to visit were coming from farther and farther away.

"How long will you be gone?" I asked casually.

"Not too long—just three months."

"*Just* three months!" I gasped. It seemed an awfully long haul to me at the time, but his opportunity quieted my misgivings. *It's for experience,* I told myself. *It will soon be over.*

The kids and I sent him off with a prayer, and I planned an especially busy schedule to make the time go quickly for all of us. Stuart came home with a report about his warm reception and dozens of invitations to return the following year.

I remember thinking, *We chose a ministry here so we could be together with our family. If we'd wanted to travel, we would have chosen something else.* Had we mistaken the track?

The following year, Stuart set off on another three-month stint in the United States, returning to tell me how he had committed himself to three more months abroad at the end of the year. "That's six months," I said. "That's tough."

We looked at each other, knowing the tough bit would be toughed out, if necessary.

I tried not to think too much about it and busied myself. I kept the children involved with a large wall map of America labeled "Stuart's Missionary Journey." We colored and cut out paper airplanes, sticking them over all the places Daddy visited. It didn't seem to bother the little ones that their dad appeared to be in Cuba (my geography is abysmal; actually he was in Florida). They missed him and loved the reunions at Manchester Airport, after which we would all take off to the zoo to celebrate his return.

"How can Stuart fulfill his fathering role and be away all the time?" a friend asked with genuine concern.

"How can he fulfill his evangelist's role and stay home all the time?" I countered.

Our days were full when Stuart was away, but now and then a sense of need would engulf me. I would sit by our fire in the tiny lodge with three children fighting for my lap. David with his big brown eyes, Judy with her clean blond beauty, and Pete with his daddy's mischievous twinkle. Judy had her hair cut, and Pete fell off his bike. The donkey died. Dave played a soccer match, and I was the only mommy without a daddy watching her little boy kick a goal. Stuart was missing it all.

After one trip, when we met him at the airport, Stuart greeted us with his usual exuberance and then looked around. "Why didn't you bring Judy?" he asked, puzzled.

I couldn't answer, but instead turned my eyes toward the gangly preteen standing slightly behind the boys. Because, of course, his only daughter was there, taller and older-looking, and her father hadn't recognized her.

Birthdays came and went. I tried to make the daddy space disappear, but increasingly my best just wasn't enough. The children would be cross. And my temper would get the better of me.

Bitterness came calling. No matter how excited I was with the work I was doing with teenagers in our community (and I was excited) or how hard I worked (and I did work hard) or how much I did with the children (schoolwork, skating, walking, reading), Stuart wasn't there. The future looked bleak.

I waved him off for another three-month trip. By then we had few weeks left at home in a year. Watching the plane disappear with Stu on board, I began to cry and couldn't stop. My father had been diagnosed with incurable cancer, Dave faced a crucial school entrance exam (it looked as though he might fail), Judy started sleepwalking as soon as her dad left on a trip, and Pete wanted to know why his daddy had to do all the work for Jesus and why some other dads couldn't pitch in. I couldn't turn around, get back in the car, and face that responsibility again.

I felt a hand on my shoulder. It was a friend, a German man, who had seen me crying. He didn't say much, but he offered me a clean hankie to blow my nose and took me to have a cup of tea. He sat there until I got hold of myself, and then he said gently, "It's all right to cry, Jill. God understands. He counts the tears."

That night, I sat by the fire's comforting glow. Turning to my precious Bible, I read, "You...put my tears in Your bottle; are they not in Your book?" (Psalm 56:8 KJV).

I put another log on the embers and read on and on. I read about Mary of Bethany giving Jesus her box of ointment—her dowry. It was, in effect, her marriage box.

I told the Lord that night that I had not been the Mary I thought I was, the good Christian wife I fondly imagined being. I could not break the precious box of my dreams for my marriage and my children over Jesus' feet. I was not that strong. But I would do something—I would give my Lord permission to take it.

I don't know when He said thank you and took my marriage box, but I began to see the difference. There was a fresh, fragrant faith in my life. I sent a long cassette tape to Stuart, sharing my experience and telling him I was waiting with more impatience than ever to be together again.

It didn't mean there were no more tears (I still cry at airports), and it didn't mean God would change His eternal plan just for me. My husband was on the road more, not less, for several more years.

But that crucial prayer, "Lord, make me a Mary," was heard on high, and the bottle in heaven filled with my tears was opened by the angels in order for God to count them all over again and record them in His book of remembrance.

It would be all right! For better or for worse, we had said—till death, not distance, did us part. That had been the promise—now it must be done. I told the Lord, "As for me and my house, we will serve the Lord."

Jill Briscoe travels the world to train Christians and church leaders. She is the author of more than 50 books, and she teaches on the daily radio program *Telling the Truth*. Jill is also the executive editor of *Just Between Us,* a magazine for ministry wives, and serves on the boards of World Relief and *Christianity Today.* You can read more of her personal story in *Married for Life,* which she and Stuart cowrote to chronicle 35 years of their "opposites attract" marriage and ministry.

55

Kitchen Door Prayers

by Holly Schurter

The five-year-old was ready to go, and she looked darling.

The red bows in her hair complemented her red jumper. She clutched the book bag her kindergarten teacher had requested that first day of school, the day we went together to find her classroom and meet her teacher.

She was ready for her big adventure, starting school.

I was the problem.

We'd practiced walking to school those past few weeks, pulling her sisters in the wagon. School was four blocks away, too close for a bus ride but too far to walk with two little sisters ready for morning naps. Her grandpa would be discreetly watching from the corner where she had to turn toward school just to be sure she made the right turn. It was only four blocks. What could happen in four blocks?

A final check of the book bag, then kiss, kiss goodbye, and she was on her way. All I could do was stand on the sidewalk and wave 'til she was out of sight. I reminded myself one more time: It's only four blocks. I shouldn't worry so much.

That didn't stop me though. I waited on the sidewalk, waving and worrying. Once she was out of sight, I went inside to worry some more.

I worried 'til it was time to go stand on the sidewalk again, straining for a glimpse of her walking home.

Worry exacts a heavy toll. It causes wrinkles, and it makes me grumpy. I needed an alternative. As it often does, the answer came just in time. During a Sunday school discussion about the power of prayer, I realized prayer might help. At least it would help me, if not my daughter.

I was ready to try anything to ease the knot in my stomach. That first morning I found myself praying almost exclusively for the safety of our kindergartner as she walked back and forth to school. I had specific requests and instructions for God about how to watch over my little girl as she made her way to school and then home again.

God answered! She arrived home safely, right on time. The next morning, she wanted to pray with me.

With that prayer, we began what became a family tradition, the out-loud, before-school, kitchen door prayer. When it was time for her to leave, we stood together by the kitchen door and prayed out loud. First I prayed and then she prayed. With the "amen" I made a silent, inner commitment to trust God with my little girl and give up worrying.

As time went by, I realized this before-school prayer by our kitchen door was an opportunity for the two of us to pray together for other things.

We began to pray for teachers and classmates, tests and difficult assignments, scary things in the morning newspaper, family members, and friends. We prayed in gratitude for a good night's sleep, pancakes instead of oatmeal for breakfast, and the way the sun sparkled on early morning snow.

Before long, these kitchen door prayers became an important part of our morning routine. As time went by, younger sisters and brothers, not yet ready for school, snuggled in and prayed with us. We all prayed for forgiveness on those mornings we had been overtaken by grumpiness; we all prayed for each other's safety through the day. We prayed for Daddy's day at work.

Sometimes we prayed for a good dessert for dinner.

And these kitchen door prayers allowed me to thank God for each of my children, and to pray for God's blessing on them, even as they were listening.

It wasn't always easy to gather everyone together before the school-agers left in the morning. As our kids grew older, they were sometimes impatient with making time to pray. Some mornings our prayer time was abrupt because everyone was running late or because someone was tired and grumpy. Sometimes we prayed in the car as we sped across town, late again for an early morning event. Sometimes it seemed more like a ritual than something meaningful.

Sometimes it became a sacred time of sharing.

I learned to pray without preaching; our kids learned to pray about everything. Best of all, we saw God answer our prayers in ways we didn't always expect. Some days it seemed a small thing, like finding a missing assignment before dashing out the door. Some days, the answers seemed larger. A friendship restored, a difficult test passed, our lost dog returned home.

Other days our prayers seemed to go unanswered. We learned to wait, to watch, to trust God.

Our out-loud, before-school kitchen door prayers opened my eyes to the variety of ways a regular time of prayer together enriches all our lives. I learned any time is a good time to pray, encouraged by the example of a seventeenth-century monk, Brother Lawrence, who prayed, "Lord of all pots and pans and things…Make me a saint by getting meals and washing up the plates!"

Brother Lawrence knew then, as we can know now, that God is always listening, even in the midst of getting meals and washing up the plates—or getting ready for school.

Next school year, one of our sons will begin law school, and one will begin another year of college. They won't be leaving from our kitchen door, of course. They have their own homes now.

But I won't be worrying.

I'm convinced God is still listening, still blessing, still answering our prayers in ways we don't always understand. I'll be in the kitchen, thinking of them going to class, and I'll be praying.

*H*olly Schurter is married to her high school sweet-heart, John, who serves St. Peter Lutheran Church in Glasford, Illinois. They are parents of eight children, six of whom are married, and grandparents of nine. Holly volunteers with Hearts at Home, works as a freelancer, and bakes cookies in her spare time.

56

But I'm Almost 18!

by T. Suzanne Eller

The phrase echoed around my house, surfacing at inopportune moments. My daughter put her hand on her hip and lifted one eyebrow as only she could do and said, "Mom, I'm almost 18!"

Just when I was trying to do my parental duty by saving her from floods, bad guys, and every other evil that lurks out there, she stated the obvious. Like I didn't know how old she was. I was there when she emerged into this world, blue-eyed and beautiful. I still remember how she felt in my arms.

Excuse me for a minute while I go get a tissue.

When Leslie turned 18, we were in brand-new territory, but somebody forgot to give us the map. Was I to treat her like a friend? A child? A woman? How could I know when she vacillated from one to the other in a space of five minutes? It was like living with Sybil.

Or maybe it was me. She made perfect sense when she told me how responsible she was and how it was time to give her more freedom. But how much is too much? What if she made a mistake? How come she couldn't keep her room clean if she was an adult?

When Leslie was just a toddler, she talked early and nonstop. When we traveled, she perched in her car seat and asked a plethora of questions, her tiny voice resounding like a parrot from the backseat.

"Why is the sky that color?" "Why does that make that loud sound?" And after two hours, "Why are you making that face, Mommy?" I loved answering her questions, but when she turned 18 and was a senior in high school, I realized I didn't have a clue about how to let go. Sometimes I set boundaries because I had 22 years on her and I could see beyond the obvious.

Other times I said no because it was easier. I didn't get away with that one much. As she matured I realized it was time to say yes a whole lot more. If Leslie was going to enter the adult world, I had to be willing to let her make some mistakes—within reason.

I watched other mothers with their young adult children, hoping to gain insight. Honestly, it only served to confuse me. Some parents took off all the boundaries and let their teens run like wild colts. Others smothered them, treating them like small children when they were old enough to have their own. There had to be an in-between. The only thing I knew for sure was that I didn't have all the answers.

But where to begin? Believe it or not, I found my answer one day as I sat on a fence watching my best friend gently lead a beautiful quarter horse.

I've watched Faith take an unbroken horse into the ring many times. On this day, she gripped the rope in her hand and led the horse, encouraging it to walk instead of race wildly around the ring. As the horse paced himself, she let out a little bit of rope at a time until it lay in her open palm. She only tightened the rope if the horse threatened to break loose or do something that would cause her or the horse harm. Eventually she let the rope go. The horse had learned to obey, and there was mutual trust between the horse and its owner. My friend is highly sought as a trainer because so many owners prepare their horses the wrong way. Some try to break the horses with a whip but end up with a rebellious, dangerous horse or a skittish horse with a broken spirit. Others pamper their horses, allowing them to develop annoying and lazy habits. Neither is able to function within the ring. "They know I'm the boss, but it's more about relationship," Faith says. "When I'm through, that horse and I have mutual respect."

I realized that my training—and letting go—had begun years before. When Leslie was young I had to keep the rope tight. "Don't cross the street without looking. Eat your veggies. Don't drink Tylenol."

As she turned from toddler to little girl, I prayed with her, laughed with her, scolded her, and molded her. She learned how to make decisions on her own, such as what to wear, how to treat others, and how to work as a team with the rest of the family in chores.

I'll never forget the first time she climbed in a car with a group of friends, and then the day she drove to school in her tiny Toyota. More choices. More temptations. There were risks, but these were also opportunities for her to grow. As she learned to pace herself and made good decisions, she received more freedom.

It became a trust issue. In the year of her eighteenth birthday, the rope lay loosely in the palm of my hand. I had to realize that we had tried our best to instill strength and maturity and confidence in our daughter. She was filling out college applications and would soon live without the security of her family as she made critical life decisions.

"But I'm almost 18," became painfully clear to me. Leslie was asking me to lay down the rope. I was still her parent. There were still rules, within reason. But she was asking me to look at the handiwork of 18 years of parenting and to trust the woman she was becoming.

Today she's 25, newly married, and in her third year of law school. Every time she comes to visit, my breath is taken away when the woman who was once my blue-eyed baby girl walks through the door. She's responsible and focused on her faith and her future. She hopes to be a judge one day, working with children, making a difference in the lives of little ones who need a voice.

And yet she still leaves towels on the bathroom floor. Recently she spent a weekend with us. I laughed, asking her to toss her towels in the hamper. She put her hand on her hip and lifted one eyebrow as only she can do. "Mom, I'm 25 years old."

I know, Leslie. Really I do.

Suzanne Eller is the author of five books, a parenting and youth culture columnist, speaker, and media advocate for families and teens. She is the proud mom of Leslie, Ryan, and Melissa, and her beautiful children-in-law, Stephen, Kristin, and Josh. You can reach her at http://daretobelieve.org.

57

The Closet

by Cindy Sigler Dagnan

It hit me last night after we got home, as I reached up on tiptoe to deliver armloads of fresh-smelling laundry to the tops of the closet, that Greg and I had just watched the last kindergarten program. The youngest of our four girls, just barely five, sang with gusto, grinning shyly, waving, and finally exploding with animation. Of the three rows of grinning, barefooted classmates, tiny jeans rolled up, all singing songs on the theme "Goin' Fishin'," I only had eyes for her.

Little bare toes tapping, pigtails flying, rows of perfect small teeth flashing, blue eyes sparkling. The music thrummed. *The last time. The last time. Last time…*Her face blurred into kaleidoscope pieces, formed by my tears and the images of each one of her sisters. Hadn't we *just* received invitations on thick, colored paper to *their* kindergarten programs? My husband and I exchanged glances; a wordless sea of memories passed between us.

As I contemplated all this, a sweater slid off of a precarious stack and brushed my nose. I picked it up and hugged it tightly, sinking down to the floor. It is a dreadful oatmeal-colored cardigan, but it is among the last things I remember my daddy wearing. And so I love it. And I wear it. When I write, when I'm cold, when I can't find my bathrobe, when my bathrobe had baby puke on it.

On the closet floor next to me is an old-fashioned hatbox stuffed full of various cards and letters. They wouldn't bring a dime on eBay, but you couldn't pay me enough to pry them out of my hands. Crayon scrawls. *Mommy, I love you. YUr the besTest Mom in the whole world! HapPy BurthDay.* Odd combinations of capitals and lower case with a few wobbly attempts at cursive thrown in. Pasted tracings of tiny handprints. And a homemade coupon: *This is good for one big hug and for cleaning my room with no complaining.* Drawings. Stick figures representing all of us, a family. A printed program from a past school event. One evening. Forty-five minutes, tops. Those memories are preserved there in that closet.

I get up, eyes misty, knees popping. They didn't used to do that. I look over at a plaid skirt, suspended from a sorry looking hanger by two clothespins. On closer inspection I see that the clothespins have names written on them: Tyler. Cheyenne. I laugh when I recognize these items from the girls playing school. Each of their "students" has a named clothespin so that if they misbehave their clothespin can be "pulled," just like at real school. On a grumpy day not too long ago, I had demanded the return of at least some of my clothespins so I could actually possess them for their intended use! I have an insane desire to give them all back and just fetch my wardrobe from colorful closet piles for the rest of their childhood. This is going so fast.

I look around the border of the closet. A box with the tissue-wrapped nativity awaiting Christmas. Some family videos. A dilapidated stuffed animal. The clothes that still fit, the clothes that might fit, and the clothes in the "I have a dream" section. I really need to get rid of those.

But, oh, not the memories. Some of my girls are already getting big enough to eye my closet with interest. *Can I borrow that hair ribbon? Cool belt, Mom! Hey, maybe I can wear that!* For now, I shake my head to clear those voices, and instead, I remember those other programs, on other nights, and then choose to remember tonight's with wistful, untethered joy.

Yeah, I know. There will probably (prayerfully, hopefully, not *too* soon, though) be grandchildren and their programs to attend, but it will never again be the same.

I have this day, this program, this memory, this closet to cherish. Oh, God, may we steep each day in memories. May our closets be stuffed full of them and our hearts to overflowing.

indy Sigler Dagnan is Greg's wife and mommy of Eden, Emmy, Ellie, and Elexa. She is a popular speaker and writer whose books include *Who Got Peanut Butter On My Daily Planner?* and *Chocolate Kisses for Couples.* She is thrilled by her twice-weekly Starbucks treats when she has to go to town.

58

A Harvest of Satisfaction

by Cheryl Eliason

The pomp and circumstance is over…my son just graduated. The cumulative stress of planning and the sheer volume of time spent at final events has also ended. In a span of three weeks, I attended the last choir concert, year-end honors celebration, track banquet, sectional and State track meets, graduation, and finally, an open house celebrating Evan's graduation. I expected to cry more. After all, for weeks building up to this finale, several moms have commiserated about the anticipated tears at this ending. But for me, the tears didn't come. In retrospect, I was surprised. How *come* I'm not crying?

The morning after the open house, where more than 200 family members and friends stopped by to well wish and congratulate my son, I sat looking at his awards and picture boards that had been created for this celebration. The baby, the boy, the teenager, and now the young man. The picture boards attempt to capture an 18-year journey of development, family fun, memories, activities, and accomplishments. I get misty eyed seeing that darling, dimple-cheeked little boy with chocolate cake all over his face to the contrasting photo of a sophisticated young man playing his string bass in his tuxedo. I marvel at how pictures capture his personality—the impish grin of the toddler peering out of a cupboard, the undaunted five-year-old hanging upside down from a branch...the freckle-faced little boy exuberant and excited to get his first guitar...the long-haired teenager jamming and scream/singing with his band...the celebratory look of getting a present...the cavalier attitude of a teen...the all-dressed-up handsome young man at his senior prom...the determined runner, competing to win. It has been a great 18 years—rich with memories I will cherish forever. This morning as I lounged and sipped on my coffee reflecting, I realized the overwhelming emotion at this ending was not sadness, but satisfaction...A very deep and humble satisfaction.

Because of my choice to be a stay-at-home mom, I have been present at those events captured on the picture board. For years, I have carpooled, brought treats to school, helped with homework and science projects, attended concerts and plays, watched soccer games, cross-country, and track meets through all varieties of fair and inclement weather, volunteered at school, and welcomed into our home (and fed) many of my son's friends while allowing their rock band to make music over the garage...loud music! Being present and available has been rewarded with many rich conversations, memorable debates, and of utmost value, a connected and respectful relationship between my son and me.

This has been an investment with priceless dividends, but nonetheless, an investment not without cost. I have made parenting mistakes while navigating through rocky moments and tear-studded confrontations. There were some anxious nights resulting in difficult consequences to administer. This is the son who has given me the most parenting "material" for my seminars. Over the years I've referred to Evan as the "Tigger" who accidentally got in trouble all day long, the boy who mastered the art of pestering, the common denominator to most sibling conflicts, the Energizer Bunny acting often before thinking. This is the son who announced to me at age 14: "Mom, you don't need to know where I'm going and whom I'm with all the time. After all, I'm 14." That same year, at age 14, he (and his fellow conspirators) was suspended from Christian school for duct-taping a classmate to a tree. This occurred the very week I was giving my first workshop on bullying. This is the son with a creative bent—dying his very blond hair first red, a year later blue, and then a trial season of brown. This son has a flair for interesting, vintage fashion, where I more than once challenged him, "Are you *really* wearing that to school?" His junior prom tux was a celery green leisure suit he found at a vintage shop. This is the son for whom I have had to learn the science and art of letting out the rope, and yet holding it firm, requiring accountability. It has been a roller coaster ride of fun, surprises, fears, risky decisions, and firm mentoring.

This deep sense of satisfaction comes from knowing now that all the time and energy spent, all the prayers offered on behalf of my son, all the efforts spent to seek wisdom on how to parent well, were absolutely worth the effort. I feel a very humble satisfaction that I was privileged to be present and available to parent proactively and intentionally. I am profoundly grateful to God for the work He is doing in my son's life. My son has matured and grown to be self-governing and is ready to launch off on his own. I can honestly say, there were moments when I had my doubts about this outcome.

The tears no doubt will come next fall as he heads off to college in California and I see that empty place at the dinner table. I WILL miss him, dearly, but I am also ready to embark on this new season with him. Galatians 6:9 admonishes us to "not become weary in doing good, for at the proper time we will reap a harvest if we do not give up." As a mom, that "well-doing" has consisted of parenting with strategic purpose and consistent life-giving and sacrificial love. When we purpose to be present, intentionally make ourselves available, and stay connected with our children, we reap a harvest—a rich relationship without the regrets of having missed the moments and a harvest of satisfaction. These are the sentiments of a musing mom…humbly filled with deep satisfaction instead of sadness.

Cheryl Eliason is an experienced parent, veteran speaker, author, and certified Family Life Coach. She speaks with great passion and conviction, addressing the "where we live" challenges of parenting. Cheryl also manages her company, Family Tools, a resource company that educates and equips parents to be intentional. See www.familytools.com.

Notes

1. Excerpted from *Motherhood: The Guilt That Keeps On Giving.* Copyright © 2006 by Julie Ann Barnhill. Published by Harvest House Publishers, Eugene, Oregon. Used by permission.

2. Excerpted from *The Bathtub Is Overflowing but I Feel Drained.* Copyright © 2006 by Lysa TerKeurst. Published by Harvest House Publishers, Eugene, Oregon. Used by permission. www.harvesthousepublishers.com

3. Adapted from *Be the Parent.* Copyright © 2006 by Kendra Smiley. Published by Moody Publishers, Chicago, Illinois. Used by permission. www.moodypublishers.com

About Hearts at Home

The Hearts at Home organization is committed to meeting the needs of women in the profession of motherhood. Founded in 1993, Hearts at Home offers a variety of resources and events to assist women in their jobs as wives and mothers.

Find out how Hearts at Home can provide you with ongoing education and encouragement in the profession of motherhood. In addition to this book, our resources include the *Hearts at Home* magazine and our Hearts at Home website. Additionally, Hearts at Home events make a great getaway for individuals, moms groups, or for that special friend, sister, or sister-in-law. The regional conferences, attended by more than ten thousand women each year, provide a unique, affordable, and highly encouraging weekend for any mom in any season of motherhood.

Hearts at Home
1509 N. Clinton Blvd.
Bloomington, IL 61701-1813

Phone: (309) 828-MOMS
E-mail: hearts@hearts-at-home.org
Web: www.hearts-at-home.org